The Lighted Heart

ELIZABETH YATES

The Lighted Heart

PEN DRAWINGS BY NORA S. UNWIN

E. P. Dutton & Co., Inc.
New York ⚹ 1960

Chapters

The Lighted Heart

ONE ⁊ *A House Is Found*

BILL was always meeting up with things that made good telling. One evening, when we were living in London, he regaled some of our friends and me at dinner with a story of what had happened to him on the way home from his office to our flat in Kensington.

"I got on the bus and stepped inside to look for a seat," he said. "The bus lurched forward and to steady myself I reached for the first upright that I saw. It came away in my hands and a little man came with it. We both fell backward, almost into a woman's lap. 'I hope I didn't soil your gloves,' the little man said as we picked ourselves up."

"Shocking!" one of our English guests exclaimed, "to have our good red buses in such condition."

"Not at all," Bill laughed. "It wasn't a fixture in the bus that I had grasped, but a long iron pipe that a plumber was holding."

"Didn't you hurt yourself?"

He shook his head. "When the plumber got back into his seat, I took the vacant seat beside him. He was riding on to Hammersmith so we had a chance for a really good talk. He keeps racing pigeons and—"

The conversation moved on. We discussed the politeness of British workmen and the amazing variety of their afterhours pursuits. It quite naturally flowed into a comparison between Britain and America with a special pointing up of viewpoints and values.

Bill and I had been living in England for ten years. Bill represented an American firm and his work often took him afield. We had had some wonderful trips in the British Isles, lived several months in Paris, half a year in Switzerland—with all our spare time spent mountain climbing, and we had just returned from two months in Iceland. I was proud of the fact that I had actually kept house in five different countries. We loved England. It was hard to believe that it would not always be our home, yet we knew that someday we would return to our own New England. But it was a far-off day. There was more of the world to see, and so much more we wanted to do.

It was not until late that night, after our guests had gone, that I realized what Bill's grasping the plumber's pipe meant. He had not seen clearly enough to distinguish it for what it was. It was not the first such experience he had had, but he always made light of his visual adventures and turned them into good stories.

The next morning, as I was dusting, I became increasingly aware of the extraordinary number of magnifying glasses we seemed to have, each new one stronger than the last. That evening, Bill seemed to put the paper down sooner than usual.

"No news?"

"It doesn't take long to read when all you can see is the headlines."

Within me, for one devastating moment, I felt as if my heart had stopped. When it went on again I asked, "Shall I read the paper to you?"

"Please."

I took up *The Times*, hoping that Bill could not see how uncontrollably my hands were shaking. After I had read for an hour, I asked Bill if he would not go to the oculist and see if he should have his glasses changed.

"I did go to him this afternoon. He said—well, he said *glasses* couldn't do any more for me."

"Oh, Bill—"

"We may have to make a little different plan for our life someday, that's all. Nothing that we haven't realized all along."

That was true.

I had known about Bill's eyes since before we were married, known that a day might come when there would be no sight; but we were young and the world was before us, and hope made us certain that such a thing would never happen. We put the possibility in the back of our minds; at least I think Bill did as much as I, for he never spoke of it. I quite forgot about his eyes until his glasses were changed, or he brought home a new magnifying glass, or a sudden bout with pain kept him in a dark room with compresses for a few days or as many weeks. In the between times our life was so gay, so full of friends and travel and Bill's business that it seemed as if the threat ahead or the memory of the dark time must have been a dream. We never believed it could come, yet it was always there: like the small cloud on the horizon, no bigger than a man's hand, that might spread across the sky.

We spent Christmas in Paris that year, for fun and because Bill had been told of an American eye doctor who had done some remarkable surgery.

Bill was so cheerful when he returned to the hotel from his appointment that I was sure his news was good.

"Nothing he can do, but he suggests that a quieter, simpler life might take away considerable pressure—reduce frustrations and all that. He asked if I'd ever thought of living in the country."

"Thought of it! Why, it's been our dream ever since we've been married. We've always said that in a few years—"

"Well, perhaps we shall have to telescope the years and do it fairly soon."

"You mean *now?* But how shall we live?"

"We've got enough in our savings to buy a little house."

"And farm?" I reminded him.

"Yes, of course. And we've got enough to keep us going for a couple of years. We'll live simply and do something with the land, something that *I* can do."

I was smiling.

"Perhaps you'll even get down to writing."

"Back to it, you mean."

Bill looked serious. "What have we been saving for all these ten years that we've been married but to invest in the future? Now the future has come to us a little sooner than we expected."

"Bill, how long did the doctor say—" I hesitated, finding it difficult to ask about what had been so consistently pushed from our minds.

"He couldn't tell me. He said it might be a few years, perhaps more. I may always have enough sight to get around, anyway we can hope."

So we went on hoping and made our plans for the future.

It took several months for Bill to wind up his business affairs and for us to make the change-over. It was late in the year when we arrived in Boston, rented a car, and drove into the country two hours north and west to a small town we had often visited and of which we were fond. It was set in a countryside of gently rolling hills topped by one stalwart mountain. There were lakes and streams, much woodland, and villages with gracefully spired white churches. We found rooms in the town, there to stay until our search for a house was satisfied.

The real estate agent seemed delighted to show us houses and in his care we looked at several. Some were old and beautiful, others were old and tumbledown; some were on back roads, others were in villages. Most of them were far more than we could afford. Then, one shining winter day, a small white house that was old and sturdily built looked at us. It stood in open land, close to a black road, about a mile from the town. A big gray barn shielded the house on the north. An open field reached away from it to a stone wall, then the land sloped down to a small valley where a brook ran. The land rose again to woods, mostly hemlock and pine with a scattering of maples.

"M-m," Bill nodded his head ever so slightly. "How much land goes with it?"

"Sixty-seven acres, more or less, according to the deed."

"Quite a bit."

"Two-thirds of it is wooded. It was one of the first farms in the township, and a good farm in its day."

"How old does that make the house?"

"About a hundred and fifty years, yet not more than three families have lived in it since it was first built."

Murmuring about wanting to see something in the barn, the real estate agent left us standing there.

We had been looking at houses and houses, wondering if we liked them, if we could fit ourselves into them; but always some reservation had stood between us. Now it seemed that one was looking at us, saying "Here I am. I've been expecting you."

Near the doorway a maple had grown tall. A row of pines stood between the house and the road. There were lilac bushes and an ancient crabapple tree. The white picket fence had a little gate that opened and shut squeakily.

"That needs a drop of oil," Bill said, turning back to the car for an oil can.

I put my hand on his arm. "Wait. We haven't bought the house yet."

But we did, that very afternoon, for the price was as right as everything else.

Within a few days the work of renovation and modernization started. Electricity and plumbing had to be brought in, and heat installed. Two carpenters who came from a distance brought their camp beds and lived in the house while they were working on it. The house was sound. During the years it had lost none of its old features though many of them had been obscured. Each day brought some discovery. Square tiles on the floors told of hearths, but all four fireplaces had long been boarded up. When opened, they revealed handmade bricks and blackened cranes from which kettles and pots had once hung. A test fire was lit to check the draught.

"You'll never have to worry about the chimney catching fire with masonry like that," one of the carpenters said. "Just let it roar until it goes out of itself. It couldn't harm a thing."

The room in the ell which had once been a summer kitchen and would be our dining room had walls of wide pine boards. Bill and I set out to strip them of their brown paint only to find another layer of yellow, and one of blue. Seven layers of paint were finally removed before we reached the wood itself, reddish in hue, but the grain showed clearly, dotted with occasional knots. Time-consuming and arm-aching the task had been, but when it was done we gazed proudly at the walls that glowed with natural color.

While we had been stripping paint, the carpenters had shouted to us to come into the room in which they were working. Some plaster had fallen off the wall, bringing with it layers of old paper. On the plaster were faint designs.

"Looks as if there might be something there," one of the men, wise in the ways of old New England houses, said.

Carefully, oh so carefully, with the aid of countless steaming kettles, the paper was stripped from the walls, layer by layer, seven in all, until the naked plaster was reached. There, on its dove-gray surface, were stencil designs in moss green and terra cotta: flowers, oak leaves, pineapples, and little hearts.

We found a knowledgeable person to restore the stenciling and while he worked I got books from the library about New England stencils. As a craft and a form of decoration, stenciling had flourished in the early days of the nineteenth century. The colors were the ones obtained from natural sources; the pineapple was the symbol of hospitality; hearts were used only when the house was being readied for a bride. In the early life of the house, this room must have been the parlor. It would be our guest room.

When we could help the carpenters, we did; and when we couldn't, we explored our land. We had been told that there was an old sugar house in the woods. People who had known the farm as a farm said there had never been any sweeter syrup made anywhere. One March morning we went in search of it.

"Cross the brook and follow the wood road. You can't miss it. It's in the stand of maples."

Those were the directions.

The snow cover that had lain thick in fields and woods had begun to disappear under the sun's new warmth, but the nights were still very cold. A powdery three-inch snow had fallen early that morning and the whole countryside was glittering. We started away from the house, snowshoe tracks recording our progress.

Bill stopped and put his hands to his eyes. "It's so bright."

"Oh—" for a moment I almost felt the pain of stabbing light. "Shall we go back?"

He shook his head, reached into an inner pocket for dark glasses and put them on. "It's all right now. I can see this way. But there was a moment—"

Nature had no chance for secrecy on such a morning. Blowing leaf and drifting pine needle left their marks, as did the creatures: two deer, coming from the woods and stopping to gambol together; a running fox, the print of the paws one behind the other. A lacy pattern, like a bit of trimming for a dress, linked two holes where a mouse had run swiftly. We could see where a rabbit had hopped, and sat down often. An impress like a crusader's cross had been left by a partridge, the marks lighter as it took wing.

"I don't suppose we're alone," Bill said.

We crossed the brook on its thick ice bridge and listened

to the muffled sound of the water as it flowed under the ice, then we started up the wood road. It was a silent world through which we walked, but at the edges of the silence we could feel bright eyes, soft eyes, stealthy eyes watching us; not in fear, we hoped, but in wonderment at the intrusion that came slowly into their domain.

"Listen, did you hear anything?"

"No, not even the wind."

In the deep part of the woods the pines were so tall that wind in their top branches would not even rustle their low boughs. Blue shadows lay on the snow. Bill took off his glasses and put them away.

Now there was an occasional maple, and soon we were in the stand about which we had been told. Most of them were stalwart old trees, battered by storms, rimmed by spigot holes, but there were some slender saplings. The road led to a clearing and there the sugar house stood: ancient and sway-backed, not a habitation so much as a little temple where yearly a hallowed rite was performed.

The sagging roof bore a weight of snow, but the gray plank walls looked firm. The door moved sideways. We pushed it open with difficulty for the rollers had rusted. The sugar house had not been used for years, but that it had been a place of great activity was evident by the legends chalked on the walls. Some years had been record ones when over a hundred gallons of syrup had been harvested; others were poor runs when only forty or fifty gallons had been made. The last entry that had been chalked up said

1938   77 gallons

The hurricane that roared across New England that fall had leveled many of the giant maples, and sugaring operations had been discontinued. There was still some equipment—wooden sap buckets, an evaporating tray, a rusted iron cookstove. A family of porcupines had evidently been making their home under the evaporator. When we opened the oven door a clan of field mice of all ages and sizes blinked at us, then scattered under the litter of leaves with which their home was furnished.

"That's another thing we can do when we get settled in," Bill said on our way back to the house, "boil down sap. It may take us a few years to get up to a record hundred gallons, but we'll begin small and work up."

We spent most of our time talking about how we could restore the farm to practical present-day use. People gave us ideas, and we had plenty of our own. The early dream of farming was the first to be discarded. Thin stony soil and a short growing season, expensive labor and no near markets had ruled it out for us.

"We'll have to specialize," Bill said. "We'll have to find something we can do."

"Something we can do—" those words were like the

slow movement of a symphony, haunting, hinting. The condition of living now was not what we might want to do, but what we could do.

"We might raise chinchillas," I said after I had read a magazine article about them.

Bill shook his head. "You won't wear a fur coat, how could you ever put your heart into creating fur coats for others?"

"What about musk oxen? They'd look interesting in our fields."

"They certainly would!"

We wrote to the Superintendent of Documents in Washington for information. Our request was referred to the Fish and Wildlife Service who replied with a lengthy letter telling us that it was impracticable to raise musk oxen. Good stock was almost impossible to obtain, the animal did not breed until it was four years old and did not thrive in a temperate climate. Its meat did not compare with beef and its wool could not be sheared as clipping endangered its life. The wool had to be collected from objects on which it attached itself as the animal passed by.

No, musk oxen were certainly not for us.

"Mushrooms, Bill, they'd make a real specialty. They grow on air and manure, and the seed catalogue says that once the spawn is established it may appear anywhere. Now, if we had a bed in the cellar—"

"No, thank you," Bill laughed. "Do you think I want to wake up some morning and find mushrooms under my own bed?"

"Well—"

"There's no hurry, really," he reminded me. "We can live quite comfortably for a few years as we find our way."

Bill was right. There was plenty of time. We were glad

for the year that stretched ahead. The future was bright, not spectacular and exciting as it had been when we were living abroad, but quiet. And bright enough.

Work on the house progressed well and we were told that we would be able to move in by the second week in May. We were glad. All around us birds were establishing their homes and the urgency of spring was in the air. Grass was turning green in the fields. The brook was racing exuberantly. Maples, beeches, birches stood bright-tipped against the dark pines. On the gnarled old apple trees near the house, that had once been part of a good bearing orchard, buds were swelling. There were carpets of violets in the woods, and one day I discovered arbutus, trailing over a moss-grown boulder. Near it were the splayed green leaves that showed where lady's-slippers would be standing.

Birds took over the air. Barn swallows streamed into the barn with building material in their beaks. Chattering together, they worked for a while, then streamed out into the air again. The sun glinted on the shimmering feathers of tree swallows as they swirled through the air. Robins built a nest in the sheltering branches of the big maple. They seemed to enjoy our attention, looking down on us as they went about their work with long pieces of dried grass in their beaks.

"You may think you are going to have a nice house to live in," the robins might have been saying to us, "but we could show you a thing or two about building."

A pair of bluebirds, gentle and courteous with each other, established themselves in a birdhouse that we had put up and set about the business of raising a family. From the dell across the road a white-throated sparrow called his high five-noted call, which Bill returned. A few evenings later we heard the first thrush, and from then on listened evening after evening to their clear fluting.

"'The hermit thrush that is New England's soul'—who said that, Bill?"

"I don't know, but I do know that the song is one of the most beautiful I've ever heard."

A strong wind came up that night and whipped the robins' nest from its branch. Three wonderfully blue eggs lay in fragments on the ground. There was silence in the treetop, and at evening a mournful chant came from the robins, so different from the cheerful roundelay they had sung while building. And then the next day they started all over again. This time they built more securely.

"After all, this is no temporary habitation but a homestead," their song seemed to say. "It must be built to endure."

Bill was philosophic about the nest. "It's just a case of starting over again with a few lessons learned," he said. "It can happen to any of us, not only robins."

We had ordered four young apple trees to set out against the time when the old ones would be good only for firewood. The nurseryman who brought them looked at the ancient trees.

"I'd like to prune them. Drastically. You'd get something from them then, at least until these young ones start to bear."

Bill asked his price.

It was cut by a third when we said we would do the tidying up.

"If it doesn't storm, I'll be back tomorrow."

The next day was one made to prune trees and burn brush: windless, with a promise of rain. By eight o'clock three men were in the orchard, climbing in the trees; branches and rotten limbs were crashing to the ground. We dragged the tangled branches to a shady corner where the earth was damp. Just as a light rain came on, we got a fire going under them. Many of the limbs that went on the fire were not dead wood. They were green and heavy, giving off clouds of fragrant blue smoke.

And the trees!

We hardly recognized them. They were not our twisted old friends battered by time and bent by weather. They looked free and even gay, raising their branches with a lively expectancy of May blossoms, June buds, and long warm days of growth. They looked as if they could scarcely wait for the burden of September fruit which their gnarled arms had once borne complainingly.

There was a queer gaunt beauty to the trees as evening settled over the orchard and the ashes in the brush pile smouldered and grew cold: the beauty of old things brought into use again. Distantly from the dell we heard the thrushes. It was well with the birds this evening; it was better with the trees than it had been for many years.

"The nurseryman said we would have apples worth putting into a pie," I said.

"Pies!" Bill ran his hand over the flaky bark of one of the trees as if to comfort it for the rough treatment it had undergone. "Now you're talking."

May was in its second week when the carpenters began to put away their tools.

"We'll be leaving you tonight," they said, "but we'd like you to have some supper with us before we go."

They told us to take ourselves for a walk and return at six o'clock. It was easy for us to oblige them.

When we returned, the house was as neat as two pairs of male hands and a broom could make it. The floors were swept of their shavings. Piles of carpentering gear were stacked in the hallway. The rooms were bare, ready to receive our furniture. But the living room, once the old farmhouse kitchen, was set for a party. Planks had been laid across two sawhorses and covered with white shelf-paper; nail kegs had been drawn up as chairs. A milk bottle with a tall red rose from the florist's stood in the center of the table. Places were set for four with paper cups and plates, and a miscellaneous collection of cutlery. The first real fire was blazing on the hearth. The smell of bacon was in the air, pancakes were coming off the griddle, the coffeepot was at the boil.

The carpenters welcomed us to the table and we sat down to the first meal in our new-old house.

"It's been a nice house to work in," one of them said.

"We hope you'll be very happy in it," the other added.

It was after ten when the carpenters put their paraphernalia in their truck, threw their camp beds on top, and drove off. We went back into the living room, now quite bare except for the rose in the milk bottle standing on a window sill.

. Bill looked at the pale green woodwork, at the wallpaper with its tiny old-fashioned pattern, the four windows—each with its twenty-four small panes, the high mantel and wide shallow fireplace with Dutch oven, the bookshelves waiting for their books. Then, as if we had not been through the house countless times before, we walked through it all over again—into the front hallway with its stencil designs to the guest room with its gaily patterned walls, through the adjoining bathroom and out into the north hallway from which the door that would be the one most often used opened. Off the hallway was a small study with waiting shelves, across from it was a compact kitchen that had once been the old pantry. From it a step led down into the dining room with the pine paneled walls, fireplace with inset granite mantel and recessed arch, china cupboard and narrow shelves.

"Remember the day, Bill, when I told the men I wanted some shelves for our pewter?"

"I do, and one of them said to leave him alone for a while and he'd dream up something."

"And so he did. They're exactly right, those shelves."

We went up the steeply rising stairs that led out of the north hallway. A dormer let into the roof on one side had given us space for a bathroom and additional windows in each of the two bedrooms. Bill's was on the west and had a tiny fireplace. There were sloping ceilings and eaves cupboards; the brown and buff wallpaper had been copied, so we had been told, from an old tea caddy. My room was on the east. The yellow wallpaper was gay with brick-red and delft-blue flowers. From the room a low door led into a loft that would someday be my writing room. I thought of the room in *Pilgrim's Progress* "whose window opened toward the sun-rising; the name of the chamber was Peace."

"I shall always be able to see it," Bill said, "whatever happens."

"Why, Bill, what do you mean—" and then I remembered. It was the cloud on the horizon, the cloud that might one day obscure our sky. And then again it might not.

We went downstairs, through the dining room and down another step to the porch with its three open sides —east, north, and south. It was a dark night, and very still. Even the thrushes had ceased their fluting. There was little to be seen. Beyond the field the land sloped away to the brook, then rose to meet the line of tree-clad hills locally called "mountains." It was too dark to see even their outine against the eastern sky, but I knew it well—rounded and gentle as were all the contours in this countryside.

"The hills are beautiful tonight," Bill said.

"Can you see them?"

"Yes—" he paused. "Or perhaps it's just because I know they're there."

The next day our furniture arrived. It had fitted comfortably into an English flat; now it seemed equally at home in a small New England house. Rugs were put down, beds set up, china unpacked, curtains hung, books placed on shelves. By the end of a week we felt quite settled.

While dusting the desk drawers, I came upon a slip of paper. "Bill," I called, "look! Here's a list we made when we were first married—years and years ago—all the things we thought our sometime home in the country should have!"

We read the list—

> old farm with small house and large barn
> fields for grazing stock
> woodland
> brook
> nearby hills and lakes
> walking distance to a village
> good road
> four-season year

"We've got everything, except a name for the place."

"It will probably name itself," Bill said, "most things do."

One day Bill was raking loam over a place where our garden was to be. I was picking out stones and putting them in a wheelbarrow. He was whistling an old Scotch air. Some of the words skipped through my mind—

> To be with thee in Hieland shiel
> Is worth the lands o' Castlecary.

"Bill, do you remember the shepherd's shieling on the Isle of Skye and the old man who said to us—" I stopped picking stones out of the loam. Bill stopped raking. We stared at each other.

"Shieling!" we exclaimed, and whichever one said it first we never knew.

We looked it up in the dictionary to be sure that it meant what we thought it did: "a little house in the clearing, a protecting place where one may be shielded or sheltered from the weather." The history of the word went from the Gaelic to the Icelandic, and its roots were in the word shield, because a shield was once a kind of shelter.

"Don't you suppose," a friend asked, "that somewhere along the way there's a connection between shieling and the French *ciel*, and then ceiling?"

Another friend told us of a folk song she remembered her Swedish aunt singing to her when she was a little girl.

"O, det är så kalt, så kalt, jag fryser, Mina kläder knappast skyla mig," she repeated softly. "It tells about a little beggar girl who is so cold that she says her clothes scarcely shield her. *Skyla* doesn't look like shieling but it sounds very much like it. I don't remember hearing it anywhere except in that song, but my aunt says it is quite commonly used to mean shield or protect."

The house had named itself, as Bill had said it would. And the name meant something special to us: it meant that whatever might happen we had a shield and shelter. Knowing that, the word "whatever" could not stop my heart as it once had had the power to do.

TWO ⁊ *The First Summer*

"MAKE the most of the time that remains," the doctor in Paris had said to Bill.

Now that the house was settled—every inch of which Bill knew as he did our familiar furniture—I was eager to have the garden take shape so he would know it too.

Dan, our farmer-neighbor who lived down the road, came to plow up a fifty-foot square for our vegetable garden. "Your soil is light," he commented, "but it will warm up early in the spring and drain well. You'll have to keep adding humus to it to offset what you take from the ground."

"When should we do that?" Bill asked.

"In the fall generally, but I'll harrow in some barnyard dressing tomorrow to help things on a bit. What's that, first cousin to a woodchuck?" he pointed to the Scottish terrier who had been given to us a few days before.

"Indeed not," I exclaimed, "that's Bonnibel! She'll be the terror of any woodchuck who tries to raid our garden."

"She better be. They can do a lot of damage once a garden starts to bear."

"How soon can we plant?"

"Wait until Memorial Day for the vegetables. There's not much chance of frost after that and it's a good way to spend the day. But flowers, you can get them in any time."

On the east side of the house were the vestiges of an old garden, long uncared for, but a garden all the same, matted with grass, tangled with weeds; in it spears of phlox and lupin and bleeding heart were bravely trying to make an appearance. We dug them up and reset them. They were meager things, but once given living room could be trusted to grow. Dan added to the ancient plants with some perennials from his garden.

"Might as well give them to you as throw them away," he said.

"What are they all?"

"Day lilies, usual color, yellow-to-orange, they'll spread and take over all the space you give them. Iris corms, wrong time of year to reset them according to the books, but most things will grow if you give them plenty of water when you dig them. A peony root, don't know whether it's pink or red, but color won't matter in your kind of a garden. Bee balm. A clump of pinks, they're spicy when the sun gets on them. Here's a columbine, you'll want it for the hummingbirds. My wife sent you this sweet geranium, but you'll have to bring it indoors before winter."

Dan left us with riches we had not dreamed of having.

After we had tucked the plants in, firmed the earth

around them and watered it down, we went down to the brook with basket and spade. A rose was growing there that we wanted for the garden. It had been wild for many years, but not when it was first planted. Once upon a time someone had made a garden there in newly cleared land where now the murmur of pine and hemlock answered the murmur of the brook. It was the kind of rose that the first New England settlers had brought with them, tending the roots through the long voyage as carefully as they did their furniture and china. Golden-centered with widely opened pink petals when blooming, it was the Tudor rose that we had seen so often in England, not only in gardens but on paneled walls and plaster ceilings.

When we returned from the brook, we noticed that there was a flat box on the wall near the gate. Bonnibel barked sharply, as if to tell us that someone had been and gone again. Bill went to get it. In it were half a dozen seedlings comfortably embraced by damp earth.

"Delphinium," Bill said. "It must be that white variety Dan said he was raising. Told me yesterday he wanted us to have some as soon as we had a place ready."

We set the rose in the garden, then the seedlings, tamping the earth down well. Just as we finished, Dan came strolling across the grass.

"Figured you could use a few," he said, then he nodded as if he were seeing future bloom, "they'll look all right in your kind of a garden."

"What do you mean, Dan, when you say our 'kind of a garden'?"

Dan sat down on the old millstone that made one of the corners of our garden. "Well, I'll tell you."

Bill turned the hose off and sat down on the grass beside me.

"There was a party moved into one of the big old houses around here that had stood empty for a while," Dan began. "Guess they had more money than ideas for when they fixed up the old flower garden they had to get someone in from outside to do it for them."

"A landscape architect?"

Dan nodded. "That's what they called her. She got that garden all arranged just so. The heights were right so no flower would hide any other flower. The blooming times were right so from May right through to frost there'd always be something pretty."

"What were some of the flowers?" I asked.

"Like what you've got, most of them. I knew their faces all right but I couldn't have recognized one of them by the names she gave them. I remember how careful she was about their colors because I'd just brought up a load of loam and I heard her explain how they were all arranged to blend and balance, not clash or startle. 'Eye-pleasing' was what she called it. 'I hope the bees won't mix things up for you,' I said when I dumped the loam. She looked at me as if she wished I was under that loam."

Dan knocked out his pipe on the millstone.

"What happened?" I asked.

"It was a great year for honey."

"But what happened to the garden?"

"Prettiest garden you've ever seen by the end of the summer. All kinds of color, all kinds of bloom, just a-rioting together." Dan got up, but before he left he had a word of warning for us. "You know," he said, "some folks want things to happen according to plan, but Nature's got a few ideas of her own."

I shook the earth out of the flat which had held the seedlings and handed it back to Dan.

"I don't need it and you probably can use it," he said,

"starting out new as you are. It's just a homemade thing that I knocked together. Put something in it sometime when you want to divide a clump, and pass it on to someone else."

We shook earth-grimed hands and Dan went on his way. At the gate he turned and called back to us, "Don't work so hard that you haven't any time left to enjoy. What you don't do this year, you can next."

But could we?

Dan did not know that we were working against time. Bill rarely said anything, nor did I. We both had hope to live on, and somehow that invisible bread tasted better when eaten without the accompaniment of words.

We sat on the long step of the porch and contemplated our flower garden. It said nothing of garden books and seed catalogues, but it told of the house's former inhabitants and a neighbor's sharing.

"Bill, it reminds me of that quilt Hannah has had in her family for three generations—remember? All those squares, each one embroidered with a line of Scripture or a familiar saying in the handwriting of the giver."

"M-m, twice warm it must be."

"And twice beautiful our garden will be, with itself and its memories."

Memorial Day was sunny and warm. We planted our vegetable garden according to a plan Bill had made on a big piece of paper. Knowing that the seeds could be relied on to do their own growing, we felt serenely happy when we put our tools away in the barn late that afternoon.

Our serenity lasted for ten days, then came an awakening to some facts of nature which we had not taken into consideration. As the green blades of corn appeared above the ground, crows came and went down the rows, nipping every other blade and flying off with raucous cries, full bellies, and flapping wings. The following day, just as the sun came over the mountains, the crows descended again on the garden. Because the onions bore a resemblance to corn, they pulled them, looked at them, left them, then flew off with even harsher sounds because their bellies were not full.

Corn was replanted. Onions were reset. This time we strung lines across and around the garden from which fluttered strips of white cloth until it looked like a small-scale regatta with all vessels immobilized.

When we had sowed the peas, they had looked like necklaces of tawny beads lying on the earth; but they came up as sparse as if a miser's hand had held the seeds. And so we made our first acquaintance with cutworms and thereafter learned to sprinkle wood ash or broken egg shell on the ground to discourage them. When we set out tomato plants and cabbage, pepper and broccoli, we took no chances. Bill made neat little collars out of tar paper which went around the plants and into the ground to protect them until the cutworms had gone through their metamorphosis and become harmless blue butterflies hovering over the garden.

The sight of one fat woodchuck lumbering across the field and looking, as John Burroughs said, like an animated hot water bottle, was enough for our valiant Scot. Bonnibel gave instant and noisy chase. She never caught up with a woodchuck but she must have instilled such terror into them that they lost all desire to contest her garden rights.

We hoed and hilled and weeded. Row after row of vegetables appeared, led by the redoubtable radish, and marched boldly into summer. Often there were contending forces that we had not counted on—a too heavy rain, a too long spell of drought, a wandering cow who took one good bite from each of our six cabbage plants and then sat down for better digestion in the melons. But, once the seedlings took hold, nothing could stop their progress. The summer days lengthened. Heat lay over the land. Cicadas sang. Birds became silent. The garden grew beyond the stage of needing our help. Day after day it offered us its bounty. Late summer found us rich in vegetables: to eat, to give away, to can against the winter.

An assortment of odd tools left in the barn had been the basis of our gardening equipment. Now we discovered a need for a crowbar, and an edger for the lawn.

"Might be able to pick them up at an auction," Bill said hopefully, "and this is the season for auctions."

"There's one this Saturday," I said. "I read about it last night in the local paper."

With Bonnibel and a picnic luncheon, we set off Saturday morning for the town some twenty miles distant where the auction was being held. Following road signs and those made by the auctioneer we finally arrived at an ancient weathered-wood house. Outside it were piles of furniture and the things that had meant living through the years. My heart ached at the sight of all those once-loved and cared-for possessions now lying helter-skelter on the ground.

"Oh, Bill, it makes me feel so sad. I almost wish we hadn't come—"

"Look at the house."

I did, more closely. The house had an empty impersonal aspect, as if the life it once knew had gone from it and it no longer cared. The auction was well under way when we arrived so we slid into seats in the back row of chairs that had been set out on the grass.

The auctioneer stood on the front steps of the house

and held up one article after another, or stood beside something too big to lift and placed a hand upon it. A small table was evidently not too heavy to hold up. "Eighteen," he was saying, "who'll make it nineteen?"

Someone apparently did for the auctioneer turned apologetically to a man in the front row. "She just did that to block you, sir. I know she really wants you to have it. Make it twenty?"

The man did, with a movement of his head.

"Twenty!" The auctioneer shouted and the bidding went on.

A woman sitting next to me put her hand up to her head as if to straighten her hat. The auctioneer caught her signal and raised the figure.

When the bid got up to thirty, the auctioneer addressed himself to the man in the front row who had been indicating his interest. "I want you to have it, sir. Honest as I am, I say that. But what am I to do if that lady wants it too?"

I was wary of moving so much as an eyebrow. Bill whispered to me that he was going to tie Bonnibel to a tree in the orchard and slid out of his seat cautiously.

The auctioneer's voice went on. "What you bid, ladies and gentlemen, is immaterial to me as long as I get home tonight. But I want you all to know that this little bedside table is cherry wood, sweet and sound, and that you couldn't buy it today for—"

I turned to see where Bill had gone and then was afraid to turn myself back again until the bidding got more lively. When it reached sixty-five, the auctioneer started to let it go. At the second "going" he suddenly pointed his hand out over the crowd, holding the table up high.

"Ladies and gentlemen, do you see what I see? There's a man in the orchard trying to steal some apples. Look at him! He's pretending to tie a dog to a tree, but while I'm working hard to get what I can for the owners of this beautiful old house, he's trying to get something for nothing!"

The crowd, some tittering, some laughing openly, turned back from the spectacle they had seen and the auctioneer went on. "Well, those apples are green and he'll get a stomach-ache while someone here will get a cherry table. Pay no attention to him, my good people. Who'll make it seventy?"

The diversion had given new vigor to the bidding for by the time Bill crept back to his seat beside me the auctioneer had got the table up to eighty-seven, and then he let it go.

A child's high chair came next, going for only a few dollars.

"I don't see any garden tools anywhere," Bill said to me. "They must have gone earlier this morning."

"S-sh," I whispered, hoping the auctioneer wouldn't think our consultation was to confirm a bid on the washtub and wringer that he was trying to raise from one dollar to one-fifty.

A chest came next. The bidding on it rose instantly when the auctioneer lifted the lid and a cat jumped out.

"But that cat doesn't go with it, my friends. That cat stays with the house and when the house goes this afternoon the cat will go with it. Fifty has it. Who'll make it sixty? That's the spirit! Seventy? Eighty? You're making that cat mighty happy. She knew a good thing when she made that chest her home. Glad to know you can tell a good thing too."

The chest didn't go until it reached five hundred dollars. The back was loose. It was easy to see how the cat had got into it. But it was beautiful. Once it had been loved and cared for. It would not take much to bring it back to good repair again.

The auctioneer stopped to read a slip of paper that had been handed to him. "Somebody wants to know 'when do we eat?' Getting hungry, are you? All except that fellow who filled himself with apples? Well, one more item, friends, then the sandwiches and coffee will be ready. You can eat as much as you like for just seventy-five cents." He put his hand on a grandfather clock that was leaning against the house. It was taller than he was, as plain a piece of country craftsmanship as could be seen.

"We're selling it as it is, ladies and gentlemen." He opened the door. "No weights, you can see for yourself." He put his hand back of the face. "No works, either. If you don't want to fix it up to keep time again, you can save it for a coffin. It would make a good one. If you don't want to save it, you could take the door off and make a mirror out of it. See yourselves as others see you. It's cheap at any price you get it for—who'll give me a thousand?"

There was silence. Obviously this was a fine piece, a valued piece. A man in the front row made a microscopic inclination of his head. The auctioneer understood it and raised the bid to one thousand one hundred. No one took it up and the tall plain clock case went to its first and only bidder.

"A dealer," the woman next to me said with an edge of disgust as people pushed back their chairs and began to move toward the tent at the rear of the old house where luncheon was being served.

We didn't stay for the afternoon bidding. The house was something we definitely did not want or need. On the way home we stopped at a hardware store in a town we went through for a crowbar. By mutual consent, we deferred the purchase of an edger to another year when we might have something more nearly approaching a lawn.

"We've never seen this part of the countryside," Bill said.

I drove slowly. He seemed to be all eyes as he took in the near fields and distant hills. There was a rich ripening look to the landscape and outside many of the farmhouses was the evidence of the good growing year that it had been.

"Look at that pile of early pumpkins!"

I slowed up, then stopped to read the sign on the quart-size Mason jar beside the pumpkins.

50¢ for 2.

"Want a couple?"

"Yes!"

Bill handled half a dozen before he dropped two quarters in the jar and came back to the car with two of the brightest and roundest on the pile. "Like doing Christmas shopping early," he said, "to be ready for Hallowe'en in August."

We passed a poultry farm and stopped beside a white table that had several boxes of eggs and an invitation to "Serve yourself." A smaller notice tacked to the table said, "Step inside the house if you want dressed fowl. Weight and price marked on each bird. Take yours and make your change. If you want someone, ring the bell."

"That," Bill commented as we drove on with a week's supply of eggs and the prospect of a chicken dinner, "is something we should have next summer—our own hens."

"Next summer," I echoed. Still deep in the wonder of our first summer, it was almost too much to embrace the thought of another.

We drove slowly in the late afternoon sunlight, stopping often for a long, long view, and talking together we began to make our plans for another year. They were expanding plans, I realized, as I gazed at the hills that fell away from us into the gathering mists of evening.

Bill put his hands up to his eyes for a moment.

"Does your head hurt?"

"No." He turned to me. His gray eyes were as quiet and full of peace as the distant valley we had been contemplating. "I was only making sure that I had it all within me—even when it was not there."

Bill knew as well as I did, indeed far better, that the time was limited. Every experience we had was savored.

Blueberries ripening on mountain slopes and in old pastures heralded the first of the year's harvests for us. We went picking often by ourselves, and often with our neighbors or friends come to visit. Small pails hung dangling from our necks, or were fastened to our belts, so hands could be free. Always a large, lidded pail was left under a bush. To it we returned frequently and into it we emptied our small pails.

When several of us went picking together, there would be conversation for a while. Then, inevitably, a bush farther away, then another, would beckon.

"I think I'll try that bush," one would say and wander off.

"Up the path a way they're always bigger," another would announce.

The air that had been quick with words gradually became still. The towhee called now and then, and the whitethroat. Insects hummed. A breeze came and went.

Bill always stayed with his first bush. Sometimes he had more to show than those of us who went wandering.

There was something about blueberries that commanded respect. We picked them, ripe and firm and numerous, with reverent fingers. Humblest of all the wild fruits, they grew in the poorest soil and seemed to thrive in any weather, yet each one wore its own small crown. We picked until the big pail was full, as well as all the smaller ones. The hardest thing to do was to know when to leave the blueberry patch.

Blackberries came later. The woods were no longer places of green stillness, for dry leaves crunched under foot and waist-high bracken was edged with brown. Summer had begun to lose its lushness, and though there was as yet no perceptible change there was a feeling in the air that the year was swinging into autumn.

"But it's still summer, really it is," I said to Bill, as well as to myself.

The blackberries sprawled in tangled masses in clearings where lumbering had been done. Large, sweet, and juicy, they shone in the sun, swayed on their long branches, loosed fragrance on the air. Our pails filled quickly as we reached for the fruit, dodging briers and sometimes being held fast by them as we sought the biggest and ripest.

"I suppose you could buy them in a store," said a city friend, lured out to pick by promise of a pie for supper.

"We like them better sun-warmed," Bill replied with a twinkle in his eye.

I looked across the bush at him, then down into my pail that was nearly full. I could see all those shining black berries in bowls with cream and sugar; in pies, changing their color and their flavor under heat; in jars against the winter on our shelves.

When we finally returned to the house we were hot and tired and berry-stained. Shadows had lengthened across the grass from the tall pine trees on the west. This was the hour the swallows loved, darting from the window in the barn to wing in widening spirals above house and field. But there were no swallows. The air was empty. The air was still. They had gone.

"Bill, look! The sky is empty."

He gazed into the high distance. "So they've gone south while we were in the woods! Godspeed to them."

Each one of us was aware of what their going meant. Winter, once so remote, had come one step nearer.

The long, slow, sweet summer that had filled us with peace was drawing to a close. The breezes might still blow warm, but around the edges of our world was a "last-time" feeling. This special kind of loveliness, these rich offerings of pasture and wood lot could not go on forever. I wanted to tuck it all inside me—the wonder of it and our own deep delight—so it would last through the winter and until the year turned again to spring.

A few weeks later, after the first light frost had touched our countryside, we went for a long walk over a back road, taking a picnic luncheon with us.

"I haven't smelled wild grapes in years, but I'm smelling them now," Bill said.

We felt like bird dogs on a scent, for wild grape has a way of flinging itself into the air without revealing its whereabouts. Then we came upon the vines running over a stone wall, sprawling along the ground, reaching up into the branches of a tree. The grapes had no doubt once been part of the thrifty planting of the house that had stood in the clearing. Only its cellar hole remained, and of the many harvests the farm must have seen only that of grapes stayed. We filled our empty picnic basket full with them.

That night I made jelly, adding the jars of grape to the other jars on our cellar shelves. In the morning, when the sun came in through the small high cellar windows, it put a band of light along the shelves. The jars, with their different colored contents, shone—delicate pink of crab-apple, rich red of blackberry, mellow gold of peach, dark blue of blueberry, wine purple of grape.

"They're much more than color and taste," I said to Bill. "They're all the warmth and the fun of summer, and the memory of long days lapped in light."

"They're your rainbow on a shelf," he said.

The flowers in the garden had been blooming gaily all through the summer. A few of the hardy ones survived the first frosts and continued to bloom. The vegetable garden was ready to be harvested. Piled on the porch or stored in the cellar, its bounty thrilled and daunted us. New at gardening as we both were, we felt when we started that we had little to bring to the work but high hopes and willing muscles. We had not reckoned that the land itself would do so much.

Carrots and beets were left in the ground until nearer the time it froze; parsnips would not be dug until spring; but there were baskets of tomatoes and peppers and cucumbers that we brought in, and bags of onions. There were apples from the old trees that had been pruned so vigorously. And there were squash! Sixty of them, varying in color from deep orange to hubbard gray and acorn green.

"Never seen so many squash from one small piece of land," Dan said, as he surveyed them. "Must have been that dressing I let you have."

"What do you do with sixty squash?" Bill groaned, after he had counted them again to make sure.

"You eat them," I said confidently.

"Yes, but how?"

"Oh, baked. In pies. In cookies. In cake—"

Bill threw up his hands. "Oh, please don't spoil one of your good cakes by putting squash in it!"

I said no more. Dan's wife had given me a recipe which I wanted to try some day.

Gradually, during the next few days, Bill carried the squash down to a storage place in the cellar. For months to come we had an unending supply for ourselves, as well as for gifts to others. When we went to the city to see our friends, we took a squash along. When we went out to dinner with friends who had no garden, a squash made a perfect present. The man who came to clean our oil burner and took time to admire our pile in the cellar left with a squash under his arm. We never went anywhere without a squash and we always seemed to have plenty to eat. The squash served as barter with neighbors whose melons had done better than ours, and the squash served as calling cards.

We had not lived long in the country before we learned that one rarely left home empty-handed; something was taken along, just in case: a paper bag of newly baked cookies, a jar of chicken fat or relish, an envelope of seeds, a slip from a plant, a few apples—something the earth had given with weather and care, or the kitchen with skill and patience. It was handy to have it to leave on a doorstep if no one came in answer to a knocking at the door.

Friends had often dropped by when we were out or away, but when we returned we generally knew who had come to call by the pound of butter or jar of jam left on the doorstep. We could tell as surely as if a card with a printed name had been tucked under the mat. The fruit of the land, the work of hands, carried its own identity.

A tress of popcorn on our doorstep one afternoon had us puzzled for a while, then Bill remembered that early in the season Dan had said he was going to put in a row of popcorn for the heck of it.

"Let's pop some tonight," Bill said, as he closed the door behind us on the wind.

All day the wind had been blowing cold, shutting the doors on one season and opening them on another. No matter how we might want to hold on to summer, it was going and autumn was coming. After supper we put an apple log on the fire. Bonnibel curled up beside it with a sigh of utter bliss. We listened to a Beethoven Quartet, then read for a while.

"The new leisure," Bill said.

"I never guessed how wonderful autumn could be —summer jobs all done, summer busyness behind us. The days may be getting shorter but there seems to be more time in them."

When the fire had gone down to coals, we got out the wire popper and stripped some of Dan's corn into it. The pointed kernels barely covered the wire bottom, but by the time they started to pop the snow-white corn filled the popper almost to bursting. We poured them into a bowl with melted butter and salt.

"This," said Bill, "is what you might call a glorified crop."

The next day summer seemed to be all about us again.

Warmth lay over the world. The sun shone from a cloud-less sky. But it was not summer. There was a different feeling in the air; a stillness that had nothing to do with the lack of bird song. It was the land itself that was quiet. No longer was there the surge of growth. The long, long rest had already begun.

There was always plenty for us to do, but this day made its own demand. We looked around us and said, "What shall we do with this one perfect piece of time—perhaps the last we shall have before winter sets in?"

"I'd like to climb a mountain," Bill said.

Suddenly, in the midst of the loveliness that was sum-mer's reprieve, I felt the wind of the future blowing. Bill had not said "For the last time," but I did inwardly.

"I'd like to be out all day long," he went on.

"Why not all night, too?" I heard my own voice as if it were a distant thing.

"It's mild enough now, and the weather forecast was good for three days. Let's take our blankets and sleep on a summit!"

The rucksacks that had been on our backs when we climbed Swiss mountains and Scottish hills, walked through the English countryside, and adventured in Ice-land, were filled with what food we needed, a flashlight, a book, extra sweaters. We called to Bonnibel, and closed the door of the house. "Back tomorrow," we scribbled on a piece of paper which I tucked under an edge of the door-mat.

We drove ten miles to an old wood road where we left the car, then we started off and up. The road followed a line of white birches and ended at a cellar hole. Lilacs stood tall at either side of a granite step. There was a rose bush growing against a stone wall. We opened a gate in the wall near which a brook flowed. The water was low, but there was enough to keep a bank of wild mint growing. We drank, then Bonnibel paddled in the water and drank. We clipped her lead on to her collar, for from this point the trail rose through a sheep pasture.

The grass was short. There were clumps of pink-tufted hardhack. Sheep looked up at us as we went by, curious, interested. Their odd eyes conveyed little, but the quick flip of a nose on an outstretched hand gave brief assurance of welcome. On the survey map that we studied from time to time, the contour lines running close and dark showed a sharp ascent. A dozen sheep tracks ran in as many directions, so we fixed our eyes on the highest line of balsam firs and kept to that. We climbed over straggling stone walls in whose shade ferns clustered; through patches of wild berry bushes; dodging junipers with their prickly clutch. Upward we went to where the grass gave way to rocks, and oaks and maples gave way to firs.

The late afternoon sun was hot and the packs heavy. We stopped to get our breath and look around us. Bill shielded his eyes to see better. I turned in the direction he was looking and gazed down the slope, past the grazing sheep to the valley land. A haze that was part autumn coloring, part the time of day lay over everything. I saw the golden world, bright with lakes reflecting the sun, as I might the familiar face of a friend. Bill saw it as a friend he might not soon see again.

Before us was our own small summit, granite boulders warm from the sun and a cairn of jagged stones. By the time we reached it, the sun had gathered clouds and color. We threw down our packs, knowing the exaltation of burdens lifted and height achieved. Then, because the wonders of the sunset were close at hand, we worked quickly to establish our camp for the night. A few yards from the summit was a patch of moss sloping slightly eastward. It

offered space wide enough for a bed, with a hummock on which we might pillow our heads. Soon we were sitting on a granite boulder with our eyes to the west, eating our supper.

After the sun had set in a glory of rose and gold, we still had an hour of twilight with color spreading and fading. Distant blue ranges melted away into bluer distances, until it seemed as if the known world was clasping hands with the unknown. Lights came on in the villages below us, some in the valley linked by a ribbon of road, others halfway up the mountain slopes. Stars appeared, flickering at first as if a wind might blow them out, then shining with assurance. A breeze sprang out of the northwest and blew over us, soft as water, clean and light, alive and elusive. We pulled on our extra sweaters.

In the pocket of my rucksack was a small and somewhat battered book which had gone with us on every mountain climb we had ever made. There was enough light left to read aloud many of our favorites. Blake. Wordsworth. John Burroughs' "Waiting." When I could no longer see to read, we matched our memories by saying poems. Tennyson's "Ulysses," long a favorite of mine, was in the book, but it had been in my memory since school days.

" 'The long day wanes, the slow moon climbs—' "

It was even so with us. There were stars and a quarter moon in the sky, and the feeling of a long, rich time behind us.

" 'Though much is taken, much abides; and though
We are not now that strength which in old days
Moved earth and heaven, that which we are, we are;
One equal temper of heroic hearts,
Made weak by time and fate, but strong in will
To strive, to seek, to find, and not to yield.' "

Much later, when the embers of our small fire were safely out, we crept between our blankets. Bonnibel snuggled near us. A light wind blew over us, almost as if the mountain were kissing us good night. High in our mossy hollow we could see the rim of our world—a line of hills against the sky. Lights went out in the solitary houses and village clusters, and many more came on in the sky. The Milky Way looked like a sparkling pavement. The stars were so near that we no longer seemed to be reaching to them with our eyes but dwelling among them. Chirping crickets and other night noises ceased. Distantly a church bell sounded: ten, eleven, twelve strokes.

Now and again the sheep baaed. Small rustlings and snufflings could be heard close by. The sharp patter of hooves and the sound of breathing told of a deer running near. Bonnibel sat up, ears alert, muscles tense, a low sound rumbling in her throat; then she settled down again, content to rest on discretion. But for the most part it was quiet, so quiet that if anything at all was heard it was no more than a rhythmic even pulsing: the heart of the universe, or one's own heart, so close both seemed on that summit near the stars.

The wind that had blown fitfully through the night shifted and came over us from the east. A moist feeling was on the air, a sweet damp freshness. The morning star rose higher, brighter now than any other star in the sky. There was no sound, but there was a feeling that light was coming at the edges of the world. Six strokes, mellow and clear, echoed from the bell of a distant church. In a thicket halfway down the mountain a bird suddenly awoke. A cascade of sound poured upon the stillness, and ceased as abruptly.

It was enough.

The east heard and quivered with color. The stars heard and began to snuff their lights. The birds heard and took up the song. The sheep heard and called to their lambs. Only the morning star now shone out of an almost day-white sky. Long veils of mist were lying along the valley. The sun came slowly over the mountains and its beams reached into a waiting world. The morning star could be seen no longer.

We stirred and stretched and shook ourselves. Bill got a small fire going and soon the little tin coffeepot that was black from the fires of many camping trips was bubbling over it. We had traveled light so there were only a few pieces of bread to toast and cups of black coffee.

I held my cup out, " 'Great things are done when men and mountains meet; This is not done by jostling in a street.' "

"My thoughts exactly, Mrs. Blake," Bill held his cup high in salute to the morning

An hour later as we came down the mountain, past the staring sheep and on to the wood road, we felt like more than human beings. Some exhilaration had got into us, and it was there to stay. It was not possible, was it, we said to each other, to watch the slow wheeling of the stars, the pattern of light as it went then came again, and be the same? We had seen the darkness of night pricked by thousands of points of light. Looking over a world wrapped in darkness and sleep, we had seen that light never left it. And perhaps, most wonderful of all, we had seen how irresistibly the dawn came and how life quickened with it.

"I'm satisfied," Bill said. "I feel now as if I could see the whole countryside just as I do our own land."

A few days later the first snow of the season fell, lying so lightly that spears of grass stuck up through it. Some of the maples were already bare, but the beeches had yet to lose their leaves, and the oaks. Hourly the leaves came drifting down, russet and gold and crimson.

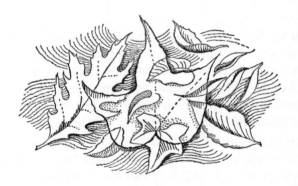

The morning after the snowfall, leaves cascaded through the air, arranging themselves in multihued patterns on the earth's white covering. I had seen few lovelier sights.

Bill saw it too.

THREE ✦ *Winter*

W H E N Bill was a young man, he had received an injury to
his eyes which had resulted in periodic attacks of severe
pain, each one taking a toll of vision. That winter he had
the longest and most painful of the attacks A dark room.
Compresses. Quiet. And time. When he could endure
light again, we went to Boston to see the eye specialist. It
was a dull winter day. There was no sun to reflect from
the white fields. The little house was snuggled in snow-
banks. It looked cozy and secure. It was comforting to
know that it would be waiting for us when we got back.

Bonnibel had gone to stay with a friend. The key had
been turned in the door. While I went to the barn to get
the car, Bill, wearing his darkest glasses, stood by the
picket gate with his hands resting on it. Driving up to the
gate, I saw him turn to look at the house and the hills beyond, then at the open fields and the big gray barn. He
put his hand up to his eyes, as I had often seen him do

when the light hurt them; then he came toward the car. We waved to the house and drove off. Bill kept his eyes closed most of the way.

In Boston, the result of the long consultation with the eye surgeon was that perhaps something could be done. If it helped, Bill's eyes would be a little better for a little while; if it did not, it would only hasten something that was inevitable. A degree of sight might be salvaged to give him a measure of independence for a few more years.

We went to the hospital together and I was told that I could not see him for a week.

Bill looked at me with his warm gray eyes. "I'd much rather you went home," he said. "I'd like to think of you there."

So I did. If there was nothing I could do for Bill, there were many things that I could do at home.

A week later I stood by his bed while the bandages were removed for the first time since the operation. He smiled at me. "I like that white collar on that dress," he said.

The doctor completed his examination and bandaged Bill's eyes again. He turned to me with a curious expression, then smiled faintly. Perhaps it was an indication of hope. I could not tell. He left the room and I followed him to the door.

"Next week we will know," he said, "but—" He shrugged his shoulders.

Now I understood the words that the smile replaced. I went back to Bill's bed. The nurse had put a chair there for me before she went out of the room.

There was very little hope, I knew; and yet somehow I felt sure that things would be all right. Physically Bill was strong; mentally he was gallant. The gray eyes which looked out on life and were as capable of seeing humor as they were beauty would continue to look out on life.

With sight, but without pain, I insisted inwardly; without the torment he had endured for many years.

Bill and I laughed and talked together all that afternoon. He wanted to know about the house. "Has the oil burner given you any trouble? Are the squash still holding out? Has Dan been around lately?"

And a thousand other things.

Among them were the plans he had for the time when he would be home again. He had been lying in bed making plans and now he told them to me so I could list them down. They began with tapping the maple trees in March and went on to building over a place in the barn to accommodate a small flock of hens.

"Wait a minute," I said, as I turned the sheet of the pad to continue on a fresh page, "it will take us years to accomplish what you've already told me."

"Oh well, everyone has to have a sort of five-year plan. We've got plenty of time. There isn't any hurry now."

"No, not now."

I wondered what he meant, for there had been urgency —not acknowledged by name, but constantly present.

"Next week," Bill said exultantly, "the bandages are coming off for good, and then—"

I bought another collar for my blue dress, a little larger one this time, and I wore it the day I stood by Bill's bed when the doctor removed the bandages. With his light and his instruments he searched the gray eyes for what seemed an unusually long time. Then, glancing up at the nurse, he asked her to tilt the Venetian blind at the window. When she had left the bedside he looked at me and shook his head slowly.

"Why didn't you wear that white collar on your dress?" Bill asked.

I took his hand in mine. I could not speak. And yet I

knew what was needed then as it would be needed during the months and years to come: the assurance that it did not matter.

"Bill, I'm here."

He pressed my fingers tightly. "I know." Then he turned his head toward the doctor. "When can I go home?"

"Next week," the doctor answered. To me he said, "Come to my office before you go. I'll be there until seven."

I nodded and he left the room.

Bill turned his head back to me. The gray eyes looked at me but they no longer saw me.

"It's good to have the bandages off. They made my head feel hot and clumsy. What kind of a day is it?" He lifted one hand to pass it across his eyes as the doctor had done when testing his sight.

I took his hand and held it. "Let's talk of what we're going to do when you get home."

We did. We talked all afternoon. I read aloud. Arms linked, we walked up and down the long corridor of the hospital so Bill could begin to feel his legs again. We ordered another tray and had supper in his room. We talked of everything except his eyes. I stayed as long as I could.

On my way out, I stopped in at the doctor's office. He rose from his chair behind his desk and pointed to a chair for me, but I did not want to sit down.

"I'm very sorry," he began quietly, "I had hoped that we could save some sight, but it was not possible." His voice was low. He seemed tired. My heart ached for him, having to say so often to people that there was no hope.

"I know you've done everything you could, and we both thank you."

"The sight had been irreparably damaged. Frankly I do

not know how your husband has seen—has got around as he has—during the last year."

The doctor's voice seemed to come from so far away that it was difficult for me to hear what he was saying. *We walk by faith, not by sight* were the words I was hearing in my mind.

"—but he will not suffer any more pain."

"No more pain?"

The doctor shook his head. I felt myself breathing more easily.

"Sometimes we can tell people that though there seems little hope, they must not lose faith. Miracles happen. But—" he stopped abruptly.

I wondered if I had heard, or if I guessed, what he was saying to me.

"You will have to build your lives now on the fact that your husband is blind."

The finality of the words came as a shock. I wanted to protest. To say no. No, this could not be. It was not true.

"You must build on what remains."

The doctor knew what I would have to learn: that the eyes through which Bill now saw were in fingers and feet, in mind and heart.

He told me a few practical things I could do for Bill, and gave me some addresses to which I might write for further help. He offered some suggestions. Then we shook hands and parted.

It was not until I was driving back to the country that the full import of what he had said got through to me; then resentment and bitterness shook me like hurricane winds. I would not, could not, believe what had happened to Bill. That it had filled me with anger against life. I stopped the car for I could not see to drive. I beat my hands on the steering wheel.

"Why did this happen to him? To Bill, of all people! Why? Why?"

Images raced through my mind—places where we had lived, mountains we had climbed. Each one was torture, for all I could think was that Bill would not see them again. Any of them. Ever. I felt as if I were drowning as wave after wave of memory swept over me. Then I thought of Bill and the depths he must have reached during his weeks alone in the hospital.

On the way home, I stopped to call for Bonnibel whom we had left with Mary, a long-time friend.

When Mary opened the door, her eyes were full of questions; but all she said was, "Oh, I am glad to see you. I've been wondering about you both."

Her room was comfortably cluttered. There was a fire on the hearth and a bowl of red apples caught some of its glow. There was a vase of deep-pink carnations with a spicy scent.

"You're cold," Mary said, "and you must be just about worn out. Wouldn't a cup of tea taste good? Warm yourself by the fire and I'll have everything ready in a few minutes."

When Mary left the room, I shut my eyes to see what it might be like to be in a place without being able to see it. I could smell the fragrance of the wood and the flowers, hear the kettle start to sing in the kitchen, curve my fingers around an apple, feel a small dog's joy. And my hand was still warm from the clasp of Mary's.

As we sipped our tea I told her what the doctor had said, and I used the word "blind" for what it was—a descriptive adjective. Once I had thought I could not say it; having said it made me feel a little easier.

Mary asked the inevitable question, the one that I knew would be asked me many times.

I shook my head. "He will not see again. There is now no candle of hope to be kept burning."

We sat in silence for a long time, then Mary said gently, "There will be other candles. You will discover them as time goes on."

After a while, when I got up to go, Bonnibel followed me to the door.

"She knows you need her now," Mary said. Then suddenly Mary took my hand in hers and held it tight. "Oh, you are lucky."

"Lucky!" I exclaimed. "Me?" Her words did not make sense, but then nothing of this whole long day had made sense.

"Bill needs you so. Isn't that what every one of us really wants in life—to be needed?"

I was glad for the routine of household tasks during the week before Bill came home, the week of perilously low visibility for me. There was a great deal to think about, and I often did my best thinking when vacuuming, or ironing, or sewing. We had known this might happen, in a way we had prepared for it; but where did we go from here? The savings with which we had bought the house and on which we had been living would not last forever. How long would it take Bill to find his way in his new world? Until he did, using discovered talents with long-established abilities, wouldn't I take over some of the things that he had always done? Our positions would have to change for a while in that basic relationship upon which every household stood of breadwinner and breadmaker.

Before we were married, I had done various small writing jobs, with dreams in my head of doing something more ambitious when there was time. Now there was necessity, and it was Bill who would give me the time. What Mary had said about being needed was true: Bill's need for me would be balanced by my need for him. Mutual need, then, was the basis of that delicately poised equilibrium commonly called a happy home. I felt as if I had made a discovery. Thrilled by it and eager to share it with Bill, I dropped the mending I was doing and went to my desk to write a long letter to him. My hand, moving fast, was halfway down the page when I realized that he would never read it. I tore the paper into bits and went back to housework. I would have to wait until I saw Bill to tell him what I had discovered.

On the morning of the day that he was to come home, I went to the florist in town to get some flowers for the house. It was February, but there were daffodils and freesia to be had. I bought a bunch of each—daffodils for promise, freesia for fragrance.

"My husband is coming home today."

"I'm glad to hear that. He's better?"

"Yes—" and then I told her what had happened.

Eyes looking at me filled with tears. "I'm sorry to hear that—oh, what a terrible thing to happen to him, to anyone." The words were fumbling, but they came from a warm heart.

I wanted to say something to make her feel better. "It just may be that the most adventurous kind of life is ahead for my husband."

Then we both smiled, and I wondered if I had discovered one of the candles that Mary had said I would, in time.

William Blake's words went with me during the drive to Boston—

> Man was made for Joy and Woe;
> And when this we rightly know,
> Thro' the World we safely go—

Rightly, safely: the words sang on as the miles were put behind.

Bill was sitting in a chair by the window of his room when I arrived. He was ready and waiting. His suitcase stood near the door. He had on a pair of dark glasses.

I can't see him, I thought, realizing suddenly and acutely just what it meant when one could not look into another's eyes.

"Bill," I said aloud as I entered the room.

He stood up and held out his hands, waiting until I came to him. After our greeting, his hands moved up my arms and he felt the texture of my coat.

"I'm glad you wore that coat. I like it. We bought it together before we left London, didn't we?"

I nodded, and then remembered to say something. Anything. The words didn't matter, it was the saying that did.

"I don't suppose you wore a hat?"

"No. I forgot all about one until I got almost to the city, and then it was too late. But look what I've brought you."

It was a braille wrist watch. The doctor had told me about them and suggested that I get one for Bill. It was like any other watch except that the crystal could be easily released and at each numeral there was a raised dot. Bill slipped it on his wrist, pushed the snap that opened the case and began to feel cautiously for the hands.

"Now I shall know where I am in time," he said. "Oh, this is a wonderful thing to have! You know, it's—it's a quarter to twelve. Let's get some luncheon."

That first walk was the longest and most difficult we ever had to make, but we never made it again for lessons learned then were really learned. Talking as we approached the outer door of the hospital, I neglected to give Bill the vital information as to whether it opened in or out; walking along the street, I sometimes did not think quickly enough to say when we were approaching a curb.

But we learned. Together.

Bill rested his arm lightly on mine as we walked and this gave me a slight forward lead. If I did not change my pace, he could tell the level of the ground by the level of my arm. At curbs and crossings, it helped when I remembered to say "Up" or "Down." We walked the few blocks to a restaurant where we had often been together. I was proud of Bill, prouder than I had ever been in all my life: he wore his disability as if it were a mark of distinction. But, even while watching for curbs or unevenness in the pavement, I was aware of the people we passed. Some looked pityingly at us; others stared. There were a few—oh, why were they so few?—who looked at us naturally, as if we were just another man and woman on a city street.

The restaurant was a sea of sound, but fortunately there was a table near the door. I put Bill's hand on the back of a chair to give him anchorage. After we got seated, I read the menu to Bill. When the waitress came, he gave her our order but she looked at and spoke to me as if he were not there.

"I learned quite a few things at the hospital," Bill said when his order was put down before him. "Let me show you what they taught me about a plate of food—it's the face of a clock. Turn it, please, so the creamed chicken will be at twelve, then tell me where everything else is in relation."

"Well," I paused a moment as I studied the positions, "that puts the potato at three, carrot at six, a lettuce leaf with a slice of tomato at nine, and some jelly at about five minutes to twelve."

"Clear enough, and it will be clear going if you'll just cut that lettuce leaf up for me."

The waitress stood near the table and watched us.

When she brought our dessert, she addressed herself directly to Bill. "I've put your ice cream down before you, sir, and there's a cookie on the plate at nine o'clock."

During luncheon I told Bill of my discovery.

"That's interesting, really very interesting, because I've been thinking about the same thing during these weeks in the hospital, and I've had a lot of time for thinking."

"Oh, Bill, what hours there must have been!"

"There'll be many things I'll have to ask you to do for me, many things you'll have to help me with until I can get going on my own, but during that time—however short or long it may be—I want to do anything I can to help you. Anything," he repeated.

I looked into those twin panes of dark glass where once I had looked and seen understanding, humor, peace. They were all there still, but lying deeper.

"If I can just borrow your mind now and then, Bill, with figures and the sort of thing I'm not much good at."

"Oh," he smiled, that gay clean smile of his that I knew so well and that had so often been like a light to me. For one of those brief magic moments of time the years slipped away, and I was back in the tiny old cottage in Sussex that a friend had loaned to us for a few days. It was our wedding night and Bill was saying, "All of me to you, darling, forever."

Yes, that was it: all of each of us to the other. Forever. Whatever.

We went to get the car at the parking lot where I had left it that morning. The attendant was a burly man who insisted on speaking to Bill as if he were deaf.

"He gives me a real fellow feeling for that tramp at the tennis match," Bill said when the man went off with our keys.

"*What* tramp, at *what* tennis match?" I gasped, for annoyed and exasperated as I was at the man, nothing could have been further from my mind than a tennis match.

"Don't you remember the story of the old tramp who had wandered on to the grounds of a swanky tennis club and was having such a good time watching the players, cheering them on while eating the crust of bread he had in his bandana? The secretary of the club went up to him and did everything to get him to go away, and finally the old tramp did, but not until he had waggled his finger in the secretary's face and said, 'Let me tell you, young man, *that's* no way to get new members.'"

The burly attendant returned with the car. Bill took out his wallet to pay the charges. Passing over the ones, he moved his fingers to a separate compartment and drew from it a five-dollar bill. The change given back consisted of a two-dollar bill and a fifty cent piece.

Bill held the two dollars out to the attendant. "Can you give me ones? I'm afraid this is something difficult for me to use."

The man looked surprised, then he stared as if reality had just got through to him. He reached into his pocket and produced two ones which he gave to Bill. "There you are, sir," he said, speaking for the first time in a natural voice, "and I hope you and your missus will have a nice journey."

It was midafternoon, and a busy time on city streets. Occasional spurts of speed and sudden stops at lights were unavoidable. There was exhaust from trucks, the harsh sound of horns, the swish of wheels as a bus passed us. Some pavements were smooth, others rough. I noticed that a look of strain had come over Bill's face, an expression he had not worn since those first few minutes when we walked away from the hospital and I had made so many mistakes.

"We're crossing the Charles River now, Bill. The M.I.T. buildings look as stately as ever, and I can just get a glimpse of the sun shining off the dome of the State House back on Beacon Hill. What a line of traffic it is! Well, we'll go slowly. Once we're on the Parkway we'll do better. There must be an east wind today. Can't you smell the salt on the air?"

Time and again, especially when we had left the city behind and were driving through the country, I had to restrain myself from exclaiming, "Oh, I wish you could see—" whatever it was that caught my eye: a puppy gamboling with a child, a man shoveling snow off his roof, the lacy shadow of elm branches bordering a white field, the long blue line of hills ahead of us. "It's up to you to see that he sees," my mind said to me as we drove along, so I reached for words that would create images. And, at last, the most important one—

"There it is, Bill—Shieling!"

"Our shelter from the weather."

The old lilt was in his voice as we approached the house. Less than a year ago it had named itself. Now a new weather surrounded us, but neither of us doubted our shelter.

Once we were in the house, Bill remembered where most of the furniture was. There were some small collisions that made me wince, but Bill had a way of saying things that turned his fumbling and my anguish into laughter. There were moments that made me want to cry: when I came into a room and saw him feeling his way around it, his hands swimming in space as he reached for a touch of something familiar, a hold that would give him his bearings. Pity sprang within me, but he could not use it any more than he could use a two-dollar bill. It was practical help that mattered.

In the outer world it might be up to me to acquaint Bill with his surroundings; in the house he knew well, he wanted to find his own way. I could help by keeping furniture always in the same place—small tables near chairs, lamps and wastebaskets near walls, rugs firmly fastened, nothing tippable in his line of march as he went from one room to another or to answer the telephone.

Never once did Bill speak of what he had lost; he spoke often of what he had and how it could be utilized. The word "regret" went from the English language as far as he was concerned; the word "plan," always one of his favorites, came into greater use. We knew that certain things were out of our life, but we were both strong. We had our own house, our own land. Nothing had happened to our dreams, or to our capacity to go on dreaming.

"I love you," he said, that first night, with the same assertiveness as when he had asked me to marry him and both of us, standing on youth's windy plateau, felt ready to accept what the years might bring.

"And I love you," I said, marveling that the words were still the same when they held so much more.

One day when I was putting away some laundry, I came upon the trim leather case that contained Bill's miniature camera, extra lenses, filters, and other attachments. Bill had said nothing about his camera since he had returned from the hospital, and I had not asked him. I could not. He had been a great camera enthusiast and his pictures had won many awards. That miniature camera had been his dearest possession for years. In fact, there were times when I thought it meant more to him than his wife. How deep had this loss gone, I wondered.

A few weeks later, when we were going down to Boston

to see the doctor, Bill asked me if I could put my hands on his camera equipment; he said that he guessed he better take it along with him and see what he could get for it. So many doors had shut for Bill. To me, this was the cruelest of all.

I had read in a book that "Everyone who is worth anything begins life again sometime between thirty-five and fifty." A year ago such words might have made no impression on me; now they challenged me.

For that was exactly what we were doing and each of us had his own set of problems to solve. This was not something we could go around; we had to go through it. There was a Chinese saying that came often to my mind during those days: *If I keep a green bough in my heart, the singing bird will come.*

I read all the books I could find in the library about the adjustment of blind persons to life, and in the books I discovered many hints and suggestions for ways in which I could help. One of the first things I did was to blindfold myself and see what it felt like to go around the house, to get dressed in the morning, to take a bath, to eat a meal. Or try to.

There was one thing that none of the books said. Perhaps they could not, for it did not deal with the disability. It had to do with the one who stood near who must somehow learn to live with a grief without end. No matter how adept the adjustment that might be made, no matter what good things the years might bring, it would be there.

We had one sure stone in the foundation on which we now were building: Bill was no different. Blindness was not a calamity; it was a heavy handicap. The dictionary defined a handicap as "any disadvantage that renders success more difficult."

Bill's first need was to gain self-confidence. This was achieved, to an extent, as he learned to find his way in familiar surroundings, doing the things he had long been doing. Often I reached out to shield him, to assume burdens he would ordinarily have borne; but I learned to let him do things for himself, to hold back my hand until he asked for help, and to keep him seeing inwardly.

When the doorbell rang and I went to answer it, I would say when possible the name of the person on the doorstep. Bill, hearing me, knew who was there. Friends caught on and made similar gestures, announcing their presence as they approached Bill. It was fully as important to advise him of their leaving. I had seen animation fade from him when a visitor, forgetting blindness, got up and left the room, and Bill discovered that he was talking to an empty chair. It had not been easy to use the word *blind* in talking about Bill; it was not easy to use the word *see* in talking to him. At first I thought I should ask him to feel things as that was his way of seeing, but I learned better.

"Look, Bill," I would say, and then describe whatever it was as vividly as I could.

Bill had always liked to work out problems, mathematical ones especially. Blindness was an intriguing problem, and as he found the solution to some of its difficult aspects he began to handle himself with an ease that looked like emancipation from blindness. My problem, particularly with strangers or new acquaintances, was to have them realize that Bill really did not see. People in conversation would glibly describe things with their hands. "Like this, Bill," then follow with a series of gestures. Or, "There it is, Bill," pointing and neglecting to tell him precisely where.

Blindness was the simple fact within which we lived. I

would not be able to forget it: not once, neither tomorrow, nor ten years from tomorrow.

We discovered ways of keeping his clothes in order so he would know what were the contents of drawers and closets, what was the order of ties on a rack. Suits had distinctive textures; age and use gave shoes their identification. There were any number of suggestions in the books I read, and often read aloud to Bill, for help in everything from shaving and dressing, to eating and walking. One of our rules was that his belongings were always to be kept in or returned to their accustomed places. Another rule was to speak when entering or leaving a room. The sound of a voice was a beam along which he could look directly at the person speaking. When Bill came into the house and called to me, I would answer by telling him where I was and what doing. Or I would try to. It was not always easy to remember.

And there was so much I forgot: like the day when I left the cellar door open and Bill, mistaking it for the living room, walked into the opening and the next moment was on the cement floor of the cellar. It was one of life's miracles that there were no bones broken, only bruises, and a rugged lesson learned. My lesson.

"Oh, Bill, I'm sorry—" Sometimes it seemed that I was forever saying those words. They were so lame and inept, even contrition could not carry the conviction that it would not happen again. I could just hope that I would remember—not only to shut a door that should always be kept closed, but what it was like to walk by faith and not sight.

I found it difficult, at first, to read Bill's mail aloud to him. Letters, even business letters, had always seemed such private communications. But I knew that I was his secretary now and so I made myself learn to read as a secretary did, without comment, and to act as directed. He signed his own letters, and his checks. His handwriting, though more confined than it had been, was always legible, and something that never failed to pleasure me was that its slope went up.

During the weeks and the months we discovered how to do many simple things that totaled daily living. I learned to cut his meat in the kitchen, to butter his bread before putting it on his plate, and to see that a cup of tea or coffee was not given him with a spoon on the saucer. We did not have difficult foods, like spaghetti or bony fish, when guests were present, and our friends seemed to respond in a like and imaginative way when we were invited out. I did not hesitate to ask a hostess if I might sit beside Bill, as I did at home, so I could pass things to him. Contacts with people meant more than ever to us, and friends were constantly offering to do all kinds of things: read the newspaper to Bill, go for a walk with him, drive him in to the barber shop. And there were people who avoided us.

"Isn't it odd that we don't see that nice couple who moved into that new house last summer?" Bill said one day.

"Not odd, really. Just sad. They're so full of their own fitness that they probably can't face a disability. I met her in town the other day. She talked about you as if you were in Europe."

"Poor thing! She probably thinks I'd be better dead."

"She probably does."

And there were some people for whom condescending pity was the only approach they knew how to make. Far better was it to be ignored.

But, night after night during those first weeks and months, I went to bed with a psalm of gratitude in my heart for the fundamental kindness of most people.

Bill and I had always spent hours of time talking to-gether—about books we had read, ideas we were enter-taining, events in the world. Now we talked about deeper things. It was as if we had ceased dwelling in theory. I was more sure of the presence of God than I had been at any time in my life before, and I was more certain of the place each one of us had in the immense goodness and expanding creativeness that was God.

"But you couldn't call that religion, could you, Bill?"

"I'm not sure. What is religion, really, but awareness of God through love and expression of love in service?"

"That brings the Kingdom of Heaven very near."

"Yes, very near." Bill paused, but I knew by the look on his face that he had something more to say. "Why is it that now, when I can no longer see the beauty that is around me, I am more than ever alive to the wonder? Why is it?"

Bill was soon going on with his chores as if he had never dropped them—bringing in wood for the fires, washing windows, drying the dishes. One after another he took over household tasks of mine to give me more time for writing. We divided the house cleaning. Bill did the floors, and the washing of all the porcelain in bathrooms and kitchen. He was annoyingly particular about the cloths he used.

"Too linty," he said, handing me back what to me seemed a perfectly good old cleaning rag.

"Oh, you are so fussy!" I exclaimed impatiently as I tried to find a cloth that would suit him.

When his work was done, there were only the most shin-ing and spotless surfaces to be seen by even the most fas-tidious eye.

"Honestly, Bill, you'd think the Queen was coming to visit us."

His usefulness took odd turns.

A knotted string that defied my eyes and fingers could be unraveled by Bill in a matter of minutes. Jars that would not open, zippers caught in folds of material, all yielded to his touch. He could set a mousetrap more effectively than I could, and I was forever calling on him to do things for me that my clumsy fingers could not manage to do. And there were often things that I did not get around to asking him to do that I found done. A squeaking door which had been wearily proclaiming its presence was oiled so that it moved silently, willingly. A bedroom window, stuck since the house had been painted, opened one night under a slight pressure of my hands.

"It's a good thing you don't anticipate going in for a life of crime, Bill. I don't know what would be safe from those fingers of yours."

His fingers had to be sensitive when he began to study braille. To learn to read it was a hard process that took a toll of nervous tension. "My whole being seems to be concentrated on a single dot, a fingertip," he sighed wearily as he closed the broad pages of the braille lesson book that lay flat across his knees. "It's as if I were trying to pour myself through an hourglass—one grain, one dot, at a time."

After he learned to read braille, he began to write it, first with a stylus and slate, then with a braille typewriter. It had great advantages. For his own notes and memos he used four by six cards with an arrangement of paper clips for speedy identification. He began to enjoy transcribing cryptograms into braille which he worked out late at night when he could not get to sleep. He read braille magazines, often under the bed covers when it was cold, and he read frequently to me. His reading was especially helpful during long automobile journeys. Once, arriving at our destination after a four-hundred-mile drive, our kindly hostess, forgetting Bill's blindness, asked if he helped me with the driving.

"Oh yes," I replied, "Bill reads to me as we go along and it does a lot to shorten the distance."

His usefulness came close to indispensability. When I began to write, often about our travels, his retentive memory helped me to recall much that I had forgotten, or only dimly saw. And he had a feeling for the elusive word. Without benefit of dictionary or thesaurus, he could bring it from some store within himself and it would fit: tailored to the exact measurement.

"Bill, you're the one who should be writing, not me."

"Write!" he laughed. "I haven't a thing to say."

It was not always with words that his help came through, or with figures when I had to wrestle with them. It was with cool business advice, and warmhearted encouragement, and something that made me continue to believe in myself when everything went contrariwise.

Life came to us more and more. Sometimes it seemed as if we had only to open our hands to have them filled.

There was no line between the helpfulness of friends and that of the world. National agencies for the blind, state commissions, and private organizations all cooperated in giving practical assistance. The government makes a substantial income tax deduction to blind persons. The post office lets braille matter go free through the mails. The American Foundation for the Blind issues a yearly book of travel coupons so that a blind person can travel with a companion's expense paid on most train and bus lines.

It was only a few days after Bill's return from the hospital that a representative from the State Division of Blind Services called to acquaint us with the services that existed for the blind. He left with us a talking book machine, similar to a record player, a box of records, and a list of titles. He explained that books—records, really—could be obtained from our regional library and would go free through the mail. The list of books, produced under the auspices of the Library of Congress and constantly being augmented, contained every kind of reading matter from classics to current novels, instructional material, plays, and poetry. They varied in length from a brief four records to the ninety-six for *War and Peace* and the hundred and sixty-nine for the Bible. The Talking Book was the first of the many doors that began to open for Bill.

We had always read aloud to each other; now we could continue that happy practice. I learned from listening to the Talking Book readers to keep my voice undramatic and evenly paced. I learned, too, to develop two reading speeds—one for material that could be got through quickly, the other for books we wanted to savor. For such time-consumers as daily newspapers, we developed our own system—reading first and last paragraphs with an eye-scanning report of between matter. However, we rarely skipped the editorials, letters to the editor, or Bill's old favorite—Walter Lippmann.

None of this happened soon, and nothing came easily. The learning to live a new kind of life put a long discipline on us both. If there were some times when I very nearly despaired of ever finding the way, there must have been many more such times for Bill. But he did not wear his inner feelings on parade. To me, as to the world, he was always his gay and gallant self.

After we had been home a week, he urged me to leave him for a few hours and go to see Mary. "I'll be all right, you know I will, and you should have a break."

My hesitation must have proclaimed my uncertainty.

"I've some knitting to do."

"Knitting?" I wondered if they had taught him that at the hospital.

"Rumi-knitting," he said.

I went, but when I returned I wished that I had not gone. Bill was listening to a Mozart piano concerto. I wanted him to know that I was in the house so I crossed the room and put my hand on his. The expression on his face changed suddenly, becoming alive and warm. Even the beauty of the music had not been able to give him, just then, what companionship could.

He said nothing, but that night before we went up to bed he remarked, "I suppose that the recipe for continuity in living is always to have a few unfulfilled things in your life. Then, as the days and years go on, actively do something to see that they are fulfilled."

I pondered the thought for an overlong moment.

"Nothing very serious," he laughed, "just something I was thinking about this afternoon."

FOUR ⟡ *Spring Comes Slowly*

A L L around us the land was deeply covered from winter's many snowstorms. It was a white world, except for the blue shadows that lay under the trees. Sometimes a bird flashed across it; sometimes a red squirrel came darting from the woods, his tail held high like a question mark; or a gray squirrel, traveling more slowly.

Standing by the window in the early morning, I would describe the day to Bill as vividly as I could, tell him of the birds that were coming to the feeder and the antics of the visiting squirrels. Rufus and Sambo they had become to us, and at times their movements were so mercurial that I found it almost impossible to keep up a competent commentary.

"What's Rufus up to now?" Bill asked.

"He's after those little frozen apples that have been dangling from one of the old apple trees—he's tearing them apart—stuffing his cheeks full—oh, look at him!"

73

"What is it?"

"He's going to the robins' old nest in the maple, and it looks—yes, it looks as if he were hiding his bits of apple in it. That's probably where he puts all the things he raids from the bird tray. He's squatting on a branch like a housewife arranging a cupboard. Listen!" Even through the window glass we could hear the chatty conversation Rufus was having with himself.

Then Sambo lumbered across the snow and started up the maple. Rufus waited until he got within reach, then he leaped on him. There was a flash of red, a blur of gray, and the whirling flurry in the treetop was accompanied by an angry chattering. Sambo, worsted and wiser, came down the maple and went as quickly as he could across the road to the woods. Rufus sat near the nest indignantly telling the world what he thought of all who tried to appropriate others' belongings, while I was still trying to describe the fracas to Bill. At times like this, the medium of words seemed slow, so slow.

We began to experiment with the snowshoes, once such an easy form of winter travel; but now, as with so many things, a new approach had to be made. Bill strapped his on, then tied a piece of clothesline around his waist and tossed the other end to me. We practiced to get our distance right, then I preceded him over the snow. By keeping the line taut, it gave him the direction he needed and we were able to avoid the overlapping of snowshoe-clad feet. That first day we kept to the open fields, going right over the buried stone walls and around familiar boulders. We decided to leave the brook crossing and the woods trails for another time when Bill had become more accustomed to the new locomotion.

After a half hour we stopped to rest, standing in the middle of a white field with the sun wrapping us in light and warmth. Bill was beaming. "I feel as if I had wings on my feet," he said. "Why, we could go anywhere like this!"

We had left a log slumbering on the hearth and when we turned back toward the house the fragrance of the slowly burning wood drew us like an invisible hand.

"Wood burning seems to be just about the only thing you can really smell in the winter," I said. "Birch, apple, maple, elm—the smoke is as distinctive as the bark."

"I smell snow."

"Snow?" The air was damp and the wind came from the east, but it smelled the same to me as any wind at that time of year: cold.

Snow fell that night and the morning world was freshly white. Birds clustered around our feeder. The red squirrel chattered from the edge of the robins' nest. But it was the first week in March and by midmorning the sun was warm, almost hot. The weather followed no predictable pattern, for that night it rained and before dawn the temperature dropped sharply. When the sun shone again it was on a world encased in ice. Every least twig, every branch, as well as the picket fence and the bushes that rose out of the snow were glittering, impregnable.

It was a hard morning for the birds. A flock of evening grosbeaks huddled in one of the apple trees. The cheerful chickadees were nowhere to be seen. Rufus did not venture from his snug secret hole. Bill freed the bird tray from ice and filled it with seed and suet.

An ice storm lays a hand of stillness on the world until the sun starts to free limbs and branches, and noisily they begin to shake off the glassy weight under which they have bowed. Birds came then in swift relays to the feeder, but soon we realized that we were not the only ones who had made food available. From high up in the maple there sounded a thin twittering. Two evening grosbeaks were perched on the robins' nest, devouring the provender that had been stored there. Flying back to join the flock in the apple tree, others took their place at the high feast.

"*What* will Rufus say when he discovers that his supplies are gone!" I shuddered, thinking of the volley of anger he would hurl down from the branch when next he visited the nest.

Bill laughed. "Perhaps he put it there against just such a need?"

"That's crediting one red squirrel with a lot of foresight."

"He might not have done it intentionally—instinctively."

"Oh, really," I began, then I stopped. Who were we to question what a red squirrel did? Had not we been the recipients of years of wise providing in the old house and the land and the woods beyond the cleared fields? Rufus might not know what he had done for the grosbeaks; I wished the early inhabitants of our home could know what they had done for us.

The wind had begun to swagger in the treetops and the sun had melting warmth to it when the door opened and a cheery voice called, "Morning, folks."

Dan walked across the room and grasped Bill's hand. "It's Dan, and I've got some good news for you. Sap's running."

It took us a moment to realize what he meant.

"We've got the trees and the sugar house, Dan," Bill began, "but there isn't any equipment up there, and—"

Dan interrupted. "I kind of thought you might like to do some boiling down this spring and I've got some spare time right now to give you a hand. What equipment we need we can borrow."

Bill was smiling. "We'll go shares on the syrup, Dan."

"Right enough."

Next morning the wind was still blowing, but its song now was of running sap and an awakening world. Winter's hold on the land was over, even though the earth was still under two feet of snow and icicles hung from the eaves.

Dan arrived soon after eight. It was a mystery to me how he could always be so prompt for he never wore a watch and whenever I asked him the time he would look around him in a leisurely way and say, as he did this morning, "Well, I guess it might be about a quarter past the hour, or maybe twenty."

Bill put a finger on his braille watch. "I make it seventeen past, Dan."

"Like as not you're right."

One of the relics left us from the farm's former days was an old hand sled used to draw cordwood. We dragged it out from the barn and piled near it the gear that Dan had collected and some that I had assembled for our project: a dozen buckets with lids, spigots, necessary tools, a big square pan for the boiling, some lengths of stovepipe, and food for our luncheon. While Dan was stowing some hand tools in his rucksack, Bill loaded the sled. Making sure first of the amount of space available, he fitted one thing after another into the square pan, then made a space on top for the stovepipe. He asked Dan for some rope. Working a few minutes longer, he had everything securely lashed to the sled.

Dan stood by, watching the certain movements of Bill's hands. He shook his head slowly when he looked at me. I knew what he was thinking. Neither one of us could have done as neat and secure a job with our eyes to aid us. To the care and precision with which Bill had always done any task, patience now had been added.

"There," Bill said, as he tied the last knot, "try it and see how it rides."

Dan pulled the sled a few feet. "It's going to travel just right. I'll draw and you folks follow behind." He picked up two lengths of rope, each one about six feet long, and tied them to the rear runners. He put the end of one length in Bill's hands and tossed the other to me. "You may have to hold back on these when we go down the slope," he said.

We had soon strapped our snowshoes on, tied Bill to me with the clothesline, and were off, down the slope to the brook, across it on the foot-thick ice, and up the wood road to the sugar house.

The day was crisp and clear with sunshine flooding the sky, a perfect day for sugaring. The hot sun would draw the sap up, the cold night that had been predicted would draw it down again. Given a week of such days we would fare well. The snow lay three feet deep in the woods and we had to dig out an entrance to the sugar house. No mouse family was in residence this winter and by the time I had the oven brushed out Dan had wood and paper laid in the fire box. We brought a pile of small limbs and branches for Bill to break up into stove lengths and while he was doing that Dan tapped the six largest maple trees that stood within an easy radius of the sugar house.

About four feet from the ground, but only a foot above the level of the snow, Dan bored a hole some two and a half inches deep into the tree trunk, then driving a spigot into the hole he fastened a pail to the hook beneath the spigot. With two holes to a tree, we soon had a dozen buckets hanging. Then we waited, all three of us, in the sun-filled silence of the woods. It seemed as if only a minute, or at the most two, had gone by when the first drip came, echoing within the lidded bucket; then came another; and another.

Bill leaned against the slab wall of the sugar house listening.

"What's it make you think of?" I asked.

"It's for all the world like the first handful of blueberries rolling around in a pail on a hot August day. Remember how the sound begins to change, deepens, dulls, as you go on picking and the pail begins to fill up?"

"Milking sounds like that when you first start," Dan said, "then it loses itself as your pail fills."

Soon a symphony of drips sounded in the sugar bush. Through it chickadees called to one another and the wind sang high in the treetops.

We went into the house. Dan busied himself with the stove, fitting in the new lengths of pipe; then he lit the fire. It drew well, though the iron that had not known heat for years creaked and groaned.

"It'll do," Dan said.

Our buckets would not have collected enough sap until the next day so we spent the time working up a wood supply and getting everything ready for the real operation.

The following morning we got a roaring fire going in the stove, then emptied the buckets, tipping the sap with its coating of ice formed during the night into the big square boiling pan. The waiting we did then was far from idle as the fire had to be stoked every quarter of an hour, wood had to be constantly gathered, some of it sawed into stove lengths, some of it split. Gradually the sap on the stove came to a boil, rumbling and quaking, while clouds of maple-scented steam rose and poured out of the sugar house.

In odd moments during the day, and there were plenty of them, we did some clearing in the maple grove, piling

dead branches and spindling pines, birches, and hemlocks that had no place among monarch maples, into a
huge fire. Green needles sizzled, dried limbs crackled, and
blue smoke billowed around us.

By noon the sap had boiled down an inch, but it still
had a long way to go so we made preparations for luncheon. Melting some snow, we boiled up a pot of coffee,
fried some bacon and eggs, then sat in the snow on up-
turned buckets and ate our meal. Inside the sugar house
the sap boiled and steamed, while around us in the grove
could be heard the steady tinkle of new sap as it flowed
into the pails.

We melted more snow to do our washing-up, then we
stood over the big square pan while clouds of sweet steam
rose up into our faces. We stirred the tumbling mass,
skimmed off the foam, and began testing. It was clear,
with a delicate maple flavor, and the fragrance seemed
to have all the flowers of summer in it. It was just begin-

ning to change from the colorlessness of sap to the amber of syrup.

By midafternoon it had boiled down considerably and we were testing and tasting every few minutes. When it thickened enough to roll heavily on the spoon, we tried it with the thermometer. Brushing steam away, we watched the mercury climb—up—up—until it reached the syrup mark. Then we took the big pan off the stove and poured its contents into two glass jars, straining the syrup through double thicknesses of canton flannel.

"Nothing wrong with that," Dan said.

It was clear enough to see through. The color was deep gold. The taste was like nothing we had ever known before. It was not only the essence of maple; it was the essence of delight. The quart jars, representative of a day's boiling and some eighty quarts of sap, were precious: one for Dan's family, one for us.

"We'll do better tomorrow," Dan promised. "Before the week is out, if the weather holds, we'll really have something to show."

We did our chores: filled the pan with snow and washed it clean, left the sugar house ready for the next day's work, closed the door behind us. The two quarts of syrup, wrapped in many thicknesses of newspaper, were stowed in Bill's rucksack for the journey home. Then, strapping on our snowshoes, we started off through the woods that were filling up with twilight. Dan went first, I followed, then Bill, with the clothesline taut between us. The snow crunched under our feet. The heat of the sun had long gone and the cold of oncoming night made us mindful again of winter and forgetful of spring. Bill said that the syrup was still warm on his back, and we knew that though we were walking through winter we were bearing spring with us.

Coming out of the woods, we could see the lights of the house streaming across the snow. We could smell the fragrance of a log fire.

"Mary's come!" I exclaimed. We had asked her for the weekend, well knowing that if she arrived before we returned from the woods she would make herself at home in the house.

"Come to help us celebrate The Rites of Spring," Bill chuckled. "I'll bet she has the Debussy on the record player now."

"And a cornbread in the oven."

"Cornbread!" Dan said. "There's nothing better to go under the first maple syrup."

"Stay for supper, Dan. Please."

He grinned at us. "That wouldn't be too hard to do."

Long after supper, when Dan had gone and we three sat by the fire, Bill said, "It seems as if a new era had begun."

It had, and not only with two quarts of maple syrup. In the mail that day, sitting in our R.D. box while we were up in the woods, was the first reasonable check for my writing. With Mary, we had already begun to make exciting plans for a sometime future when she would make her home with us. Sap was indeed rising.

"I'd like to do what I could to help you both," Mary said.

"And Shieling will help us all."

That last prediction came true first.

One early spring day I was exploring the piece of woods, not our land, across the road from the house. Except for a few tall pines, it had been devastated some years ago by a hurricane and was rapidly growing up to brush. Huge fallen trees lay on the ground, rotting and decaying; among them was the impatient growth of small hardwoods—

maple, beech, birch—tangled with blackberry bushes. Beyond the blowdown area were some very handsome trees,
with carpets of wild flowers at their base. And beyond
them was a small meadow, yellow with dried rushes
and green with the year's new growing. On the edge of
the meadow stood a white birch beside a granite boulder,
sentinel-like.

I brought back the story of my discovery. "It's Eden at
our door," I said to Bill as I told him of the trees that had
been protected by the slope of the hill from the hurricane's
path, of the massive, lichen-covered boulders that stood
gray against waist-high ferns. The trees, hardwoods for
the most part, rose tall with straight trunks to tower in
leafy crowns. Among them was an occasional hemlock,
its dark mass tipped with bright new green. "And Bill, the
ground is covered with trailing pine and checkerberry. I
found the wide flat leaves of arbutus sprawling in several
places, and there were lady's-slippers—pink and stately.
It was all so quiet, then I became aware of a muffled gur-
gling sound. Going toward it I found a spring, hidden
by rocks and shaded by arum and ferns. A trail ran from
it to another spring which bubbled out of the richest,
blackest mire I've ever seen."

"Sounds like an animal trail."

"Oh, it was, I'm sure it was. And to think that it's been
there all this time!"

A few days later the mailman told us that the land across
the road had been sold for stumpage.

"Oh, no!"

"That's what I heard." He drove off, ready to deliver
mail and news to the next house a mile down the road.

"What he hears is generally right," Bill reminded me.

I couldn't and wouldn't believe it. "Why, we've only
just discovered it for ourselves!"

"But it isn't our land."

"Except by appreciation." It was slim argument, I knew.

A few days later we had to believe the sounds we heard—thudding of axes, whirring of power saws, shuddering crash of trees, flapping of startled birds. Then silence.

I went down to see what was going on. When I reached the clearing, I was amazed to see how many trees already lay on the ground. The air was heavy with the smell of resin and sap. Stumps stood ringed and tawny and oozing. All around were piles of lopped-off branches. A team of horses, picking their way through the debris, strained to draw the scoot on which were half a dozen huge logs.

The driver hailed me. "You live in the house up the slope across the road?"

I nodded.

"Nice view we're opening up for you folks."

Nice view, indeed!

But they had not reached the trees that shaded the animal trail between the springs, and they were still a good way from the sentinel birch.

"Are you cutting clear down to the little meadow?"

"Sure thing, lady. Once we get into a piece of woodland we take out everything that's usable. This is stumpage, not selective, but we won't get down to those big trees until next week."

On the way back I met the boss.

"What will the lumber be used for?" I asked, wondering if anything could be more needful than its present use of harboring birds, sheltering wild flowers, holding springs for forest creatures to drink from.

"The ash will make good ax handles, and there's nothing better for jam buckets than white birch. There's a use for every tree that grows."

I saw his eye run up a maple tree. "Too much shade," he said. "There'll be more breezes without it."

In the face of doom I felt bold, telling him of the green world between the springs, asking if he could spare it.

He looked puzzled.

"That's where the thrushes nest."

"Birds." He nodded his head.

"That's where the arbutus grows. There are springs that will dry up if you cut down the trees." By the expression on his face I knew that all my arguments were as weighty as milkweed seed pods before the ponderables of running board feet so much per thousand.

"Why, I couldn't save a little piece like that," he smiled tolerantly. "When my men get into an area they like to cut it clean."

"Couldn't you leave just a few trees? That maple, for instance."

He shook his head. "There's fine flooring in that tree. My men will want to take it down first thing Monday morning. They wouldn't feel happy if I asked them to leave it."

"Or the birch down by the meadow?"

He leaned over and scratched at something in the earth, then he held up a thin yellow root. "Like to chew on goldthread?" he asked. Offering the piece to me, he bent over again to pull one for himself.

We stood there, silently chewing on goldthread.

"There's fine ax handles in that birch," he said. "I know the one you mean. But just between you and me, I'd trade a few thousand feet of white or red pine for all this hardwood."

"You would?"

"Yup."

I asked him if he would stop in at our house sometime that afternoon.

"Sure thing, lady, at quitting time. Anything to oblige. Remson's my name."

I turned and walked as quickly as I could over the track the lumbering had opened and back to the house. Bill would think of some way of saving the trees. I knew he would.

Look thy last on all things lovely—the words beat in my mind. But it need not be so. Bill would save the trees.

At four o'clock, the sounds of lumbering ceased and a short while later the boss arrived. Bill held out his hand to him, then they sat down.

"Nice place you have here."

"We like it."

"Looks as if we're in for some good weather this summer."

"We can use all that comes."

They went on and on with their preliminaries. I left the room for the kitchen to get something started for supper. When I returned they were talking just as affably but this time it was in terms of running board feet. Bill was referring to pine, white and red, as if to a talisman. Every time Mr. Remson used the word "pine" it was with respect.

"I'll do that, sir. Always glad to oblige. Tell your wife to mark with white paint the hardwoods she'd like to have saved."

"You might look over all our woods while you're about it and let me know if there are any more mature trees that you think should come out. Selective cutting, of course."

"Selective. Yes, sir. We don't care what we do. It's whatever the landowner specifies."

"Bill, you mean the trees are saved?"

He nodded. "Some of them. Mr. Remson and I have just done a little deal."

I went to the door with Mr. Remson.

"Mighty smart man, your husband," he said, standing on the doorstep. "Why don't you both come down first of next week and see the cutting we're doing?"

I tried to explain that the footing might be difficult.

"My men never leave any axes or saws lying about."

"Even so, it's still rough going for someone who doesn't see."

Mr. Remson stared at me. "You mean he doesn't see— with his eyes?"

I nodded.

"Glory be!" The tone of his voice was enough. He held his hand out and shook mine as if it were a pump handle. "Good night, lady. I've been glad to be able to oblige you. Both of you."

After he drove off in his truck there was silence, then a thrush called from one of the tall trees near the forest meadow. It was answered by another. And another, until the air was alive with their fluting. To me the sound was like a paean of victory—or gratitude. Perhaps it was both.

Then I realized the cost: some trees that did not belong to us had been saved at the expense of our own pines.

"Bill, what does it mean, this deal you've made? How far is it apt to go?"

"Mr. Remson convinced me of the practicality of harvesting mature trees as a crop. They reach a point where they have no more growing to do and, though they may stand for years, they become subject to decay, to storms, to an inevitable end. Cut them when they are mature and they have a whole new life before them as floors, boxes, walls. Pine has so many uses. Why, a thousand running board feet—"

"But, Bill, what does it *mean?* Are the lumbermen going to devastate our own beautiful woods? Cut down our pines?"

"Only some of the mature ones. Don't you see what it means? This place we love is working for us. Those trees, cut and sawed are money in the bank for us—a lot of money. Taking out the biggest and best will give the younger ones a chance to develop, to become marketable in their time."

" 'Almost thou persuadest me,' " I said, "and yet—"

"Wait a bit, and I think you'll see that this deal is one where we really can eat and have our cake at the same time."

Soon it was our fields that joined hands with our woods to work for us. Bill learned of a nearby farmer who needed more pastures for his stock. We entered into a long-term arrangement with him to fence the land and improve the fields, for which he paid us a yearly rental: so much for every ten sheep, so much for one cow. Soon we were enjoying the near presence of a flock of sheep and a herd of heifers. The field east of the house that was flat and stone-free was improved for hay. Each year a better crop, a cash crop for us, would be taken from it.

It was exactly as Bill had predicted: the place itself was helping us.

"Don't go at it, go around it," I had heard Dan say when some digging was being done and a stone was encountered. Prodding exploratively round and round, the crowbar did its work and the stone was pried out. During those first years, as we got used to a new way of living, the constant call to us was not to go "at" a thing but to go "around" it.

We boarded off a small section of the barn for a flock of hens and bought seven ready-to-lay pullets who soon made themselves at home. We divided their care between us, though Bill often did it all. He went over to them in the morning, his way made clear by the flagstone walk that linked house to barn, to fill their trough with mash and give them fresh water. His movements were so unhurried that the hens welcomed his presence. I would clean their dropping board. Bill gathered the eggs from the nests in the late afternoon and gave the hens their daily treat of scratch grain.

With the ardor of pullets they laid eggs of all sizes, double yolkers, triple yolkers, and sometimes little peewees. But by early summer they settled down to producing eggs that were even in size. Simple as their care was, they repaid it in countless ways. The greeting they gave Bill in the morning was one of the joys of his day, as was their soothing sleepy cooing the last thing at night. Their delight over their afternoon corn, or some tidbit from the garden, was gratifying, as was their contented clucking heard throughout the day. With a crescendo of enthusiasm they announced their eggs. We heard them, whether we were in the house or the garden, and would say pridefully, "There's another egg!" We used all that we could, and any extra ones I put down cellar in a crock filled with water glass against the winter.

"Feed them right, keep them clean," was the only advice we were ever given. It proved sufficient, until one day a handsome copper-hued bird appeared to be ailing.

"She looks miserable," I reported to Bill. "She's huddled up on one leg in a corner of the run. She won't eat. She won't come when I call. What shall we do?"

"Let's put her in the other run so the hens won't bother her."

We did, but by midday her condition was no better. Instead of standing in a corner she had settled down on the ground and looked like an abandoned feather duster. A film had come over her eyes. A saying I had picked up somewhere kept running through my mind, "A sick hen is a dead hen."

"There must be something we can do," Bill said.

The books and pamphlets we had on poultry raising did not help us, nor did she respond to anything we did for her or offered to her. There was only one obvious answer, but I didn't have the courage to do it; so I put her in a box on the front seat of the car and drove a mile down the road to a farmer who had had hens for forty years.

He looked at her and felt all over her body, but he did not shake his head. "Are your runs eaten pretty bare?"

They were. It was midsummer and the hens now had for green stuff only what we brought them from the garden.

"Put her on the loose where there's plenty of green. If she has the will to live she'll doctor herself."

I told Bill what the farmer had said to me.

"Well, we'll give her the run of the barnyard and see what happens." He lifted her out of the box and set her on the ground.

She opened one eye, then the lid closed over it again. We sat down on the grass and waited. After two or three minutes she opened both eyes. Hardly daring to speak above a whisper, as if some magic spell might be broken, I relayed her actions to Bill. They were slow and cautious at first, but they began to gain momentum.

"She's opening her eyes. She's taken a step—oh, poor thing, she's collapsed again! I'll help her up."

"No," he reached out a restraining hand to me. "Let her do things for herself."

"Now she's picked herself up—she's walking slowly, oh, so slowly, as if the ground were thin ice. She stops every so often to peck at the earth—she's got her head up, and she's walking now as if she were looking for something. She's unsteady on her feet, but she acts as if she knew what she was doing. Why, she's eating some weeds—eating them as if her life depended on them."

"Perhaps it does. What kind of weed?"

I went over to the hen to observe her more closely. "It's sorrel, you know, the plant with long pointed leaves. You've pulled them out of the garden in basketsfull. She's settling down now to rest, but she looks better already."

By late afternoon the hen was herself again, clamoring to join her sisters for their feed of scratch. In fact, she was a little more than herself: from that time on she was unquestionably Head Girl. She had had an experience that set her above the others and it gave them a certain awe of her. We called her Copper Queen. Her coloring had always been distinctive; now her new attitude added to her distinction. We had reason to believe that she became our best egg producer and exerted an influence on her subjects, for the daily count of eggs went up.

Several times a week after that, in the early evening, we let the hens out of their run. They walked around pecking at the grass, scratching the earth, searching until they found what they wanted. As soon as darkness began to come down, they could be trusted to put themselves to bed, walking in sedate single file behind Copper Queen into the run with the open gate, up the step, through the little door and onto their perch.

It was because of Copper Queen that we got fond of that particular flock, too fond to part with them when we should, and we kept them through the winter. Their egg production began to fall off in November. They lost their feathers as the trees had their leaves, and in accordance with the inexorable law that said what made feathers made eggs, they began to lose weight. They got to be almost naked. Their water bucket froze solid during the long cold nights. Even a hot mash in the morning did not interest them as it should. But they survived. They began to put on new feathers, to lay again, and they went hopefully into their second year; but no matter how content they were, or how their eggs were appreciated, they could not do what they had done for us during their first year.

We learned to buy pullets in the early spring and keep them through November. After a time that had been mutually enjoyable, they attained another sphere of usefulness. Dan told us of a man who dressed poultry, using clean, kind, modern methods. Twenty dozen eggs I had been able to store in water glass for use during the winter; now, seven hens, nicely dressed, waited in the freezer for the time when their second appearance would be made—as a golden roast, or a fricassee rich with gravy and dumplings. They had received our gratitude all summer. We gave it to them again. As the Indian prays to the beaver he has slain that its spirit of industry may become his, I prayed that the quiet contentment and orderly conduct of life evidenced by a hen might become mine.

The hens did what they could in the life of the place with their eggs, and themselves, and that precious-as-gold by-product—their droppings—which were kept in a box with a handful of wood ash added daily for sweetening. When the box was full, we took it to the garden and worked the manure into the soil around some of our special crops—melons, tomatoes, eggplant. If there was more than we could use at one time, it was layered into the compost heap. Long after the first set of hens had given place to another something of themselves and each successive set was used to build up our earth.

Bill knew his way around the house from sighted days, and he had the image of it clear in his mind. The outside area took longer to come into shape, but in time he knew it as well as he did the different rooms of the house. Bordered by an evergreen hedge, the flower garden was almost like a summertime outdoor room. The perennials had taken hold well and bloomed beautifully. Among them space was kept for a spring setting of annuals—petunias, zinnias, bachelor buttons, and always white nicotiana. Fragrant and prolific, it seeded itself during the summer and kept appearing in unexpected places. Bill had a special feeling for it. In the evening, when he went outdoors for a stroll, the fragrance of the nicotiana—night-scented stock—was like a guiding hand.

Once it was established, the flower garden required little care and gave us constant joy. The vegetable garden required a great deal of care, but it returned it manyfold. Early in January when the seed catalogues commenced to arrive, I read them to Bill, described their gay pictures, and he made lists. The first list of desired seeds would have covered an acre of land without a doubt, but gradually we whittled our wants down to an amount reasonably right for our modest fifty-foot square. During the evenings we discussed the merits of different varieties of corn, the succulence of certain beans, the value of one type of squash against another, how much space should be saved for melons and how many tomato plants should be set out. I drew a plan, a new one each year, with some of the rows running north and south, others east and west. We sent in our order for seeds and from the time they arrived it was hard to wait for the snow to go and the ground to dry out so the garden could be readied for planting.

After the first green shoots appeared, we divided the tasks. Bill with his sensitive fingers was a wonder at weeding—pussley, chickweed, sorrel were as distinct to him as were upthrusting chard and feathery carrot. While I would be thinning a row or setting out lettuce, Bill would work along the edges of the garden where the field grass grew and sickle a space two feet wide which gave us a tidy walkable border. By late June and early July, as the garden grew lush, less care was needed. Week after golden summer week went on and the garden's riches seemed out of all proportion to the first weeks of work in it. We harvested and canned, stored, used, and gave away. Much of the early work had been done on our knees; I felt like dropping to my knees in gratitude at the bounty before us.

Squash pie ushered in the winter season, and as far as Bill was concerned he never cared how often I made it, especially when it was made the Vermont way with maple syrup instead of brown sugar. Squash cake was another matter.

Bill never saw any reason why I should make a cake

other than my usual yellow one with a chocolate frosting.

"Wouldn't you like a devil's food just once, for a change?"

"But why, when your yellow cake is always so good?"

Three harvest seasons had gone by and I had not yet made the squash cake that Dan's wife had told me about. In a loyal endeavor to do justice to the squash in the cellar I made it.

After his first bite, Bill asked reproachfully, "Why don't you keep to what you're sure of, what you can do well?"

Half of the cake stayed in the cakebox, getting hard and stale. One morning, when we were doing the breakfast dishes, I said that I really must do something with the cake.

"Give it to the chickadees."

"They prefer sunflower seeds."

"Can't you throw it away?"

"You know I don't like to waste food."

"And you save it when you make me eat it?"

"Don't worry. I'll find some use for it. I'll mix it up with something else."

"Now, that I would call waste!" Bill exclaimed. "Using good new material to resurrect something that should be decently buried."

"That cake is still very much alive, and where there's life there's use."

"Just as long as you don't expect me to eat it," Bill said with finality. In a few moments he had started toward the barn to stack some kindling which he had recently split.

That was the morning that there was a letter in the mail from Stuart and Netta, saying they were driving north to see the foliage and would stop in to see us. Looking at the date more closely, I realized that this was the day they were coming.

"Couldn't be a better day," Bill said. "The leaves haven't started to fall yet."

"But it's Wednesday! The stores are closed. Whatever shall I have for dinner?"

"Oh, you'll dream up something."

I went to the kitchen. In the refrigerator there were some odds and ends, every one of which would have found its way to the table for Bill and me; but for company? I wasn't at all sure. Taking everything that looked possible out of the frig, I lined the dishes up on the kitchen counter.

There was an end of a piece of steak, a small dish of peas, some gravy left over from a pork roast, a pimento that was all right on one side, and quite a lot of mashed potato. Looking at the collection, I began to see a major dish coming into being: cut the steak small and add some minced onion and celery, mix the gravy with tomato paste and a little sour cream, chop up the pimento and add a few olives, toss in some herbs for seasoning, then put everything together in a deep casserole and smooth the mashed potato over the top, dot it liberally with butter and bake in a moderate oven.

"I'll call it *Casserole Caprice avec Boeuf et Oignons,* and I'll tell them—no, I won't tell them anything! A good cook keeps her secrets."

Once the main dish was attended to and a salad made, I could put my mind on the dessert. I consulted the cakebox and shuddered. No, I could not, simply could not, serve the squash cake even though I covered it with sauce or lashed it with whipped cream. Bill would know what it was at the first taste and my notions about waste would seem more eccentric than ever. He wouldn't say anything before company, but there would be an expression on his face that would tell me more subtly than

words that he knew and did not approve. I promised myself that tomorrow I would give the cake to the birds.
Even if the chickadees did not touch it, the jays would.

I went to the cellar where we had several jars of blueberries, but they called to be put into a pie and I knew
then that there simply wasn't time to make a pie if I was
to be ready with the house tidy and the table set by the
time our friends were due to arrive. Then an idea began
to tickle my mind and I went back to the kitchen.

"I'll call it *Flummery à la Maison Phantastique*. That
will satisfy them. They'll not know what it's made of and
I'll not tell them."

I took the cake from the box and carefully sheared off
its one-time orange icing that had become hard and ob-
durate. Then I put the cake through the meat grinder
and soon its bricklike bulk was transformed into crumbs.
I beat three egg yolks with two cups of milk and added
this to the crumbs, setting the egg whites aside for later
use.

"Flavor," I thought, "that will do it more than anything."

I added a teaspoon of vanilla, a quarter teaspoon of al-
mond extract and the same amount of lemon, tasting the
result as I went along, and trying to decide what was still
needed. Cinnamon was, definitely, and a grating of nut-
meg. The flummery would bake in a gentle oven for about
half an hour and be served warm, covered with a frothy
layer made from melting down the orange icing and mixing
it with the egg whites stiffly beaten. Like the best French
cooking, it would defy identification or analysis. I decided
that nothing would induce me to give my secret away.

Our friends came early enough for us to have a walk
before dinner, and they seemed to enjoy the dinner for

there was not a scrap left of either the *Casserole Caprice* or the *Flummery Phantastique*.

"I can't think how you can produce such a wonderful meal, living out here in the country as you do," Stuart said.

I smiled gratefully at him.

"As for that dessert," Netta sighed, "I've never tasted anything quite so delectable. I do hope that you'll give me the recipe."

"It's quite easy," I began, "but you must always have something to start with."

"Yes?" Netta said eagerly. "Stuart, do give me your pencil and a piece of paper so I can take this down. Yes, and what is it that you start with?"

"That," I said, "is my secret."

I did not dare glance across the table at Bill. Had I seen a certain look on his face, I might not have been able to keep my secret.

Off and on during the evening I wondered about my conscience and whether it should feel guiltier than it did, for the reconstruction of the cake was the first and only time I had ever done anything to deceive Bill since he had lost his sight.

"It was worth it, Buttercup," Bill said to me after our guests had left.

I felt absolved by the smile that hovered over his lips.

FIVE *⁊ Everyone Has a Part To Play*

D U R I N G the first year of blindness, Bill's adjustment seemed made with grace and speed; at least to those who did not realize that he had been learning to adjust during the years when his vision had been dimming. To him the progress, not only in learning braille but in ordinary daily routines, often seemed slow, for he longed to be active and of some service to life. I felt certain that the skills that were peculiarly his would be used again, but it would take time and something without which even time would have been fruitless—that patient willingness to master a whole new way of living. I would have done anything to help him on his way, yet what I could do—or Mary, or his friends—was limited: much of the new way he had to discover for himself.

He had always liked people and he had the gift of reaching easily into others' lives. His touch was light, but it carried comfort, and he seemed to have the ability always to say the heartening thing. He could talk for hours about events in the world, business, new cars, books; but after he lost his sight a deeper sympathy came to aid his natural friendliness. People who needed to talk to someone about what was troubling them began to turn to him. Perhaps the fact that he could not see their faces, or their eyes, had something to do with the freedom they felt in unburdening to him. I never knew what he said, but I could tell later on by the expression on a face that something had been accomplished. Experience became a bond, and what he seemed increasingly able to do was to help another see that the hard thing imposed by life could be a source of strength.

"He gives us all such courage," a woman said to me as she left the house after an hour's talk with Bill.

I did not realize it at the time, but Bill in his concern for others and deephearted desire to implement it in practical ways was laying the foundation for a new work in life.

Sometime during the second summer an unusual opportunity came to Bill, and he was eager to accept it. He was asked to teach business organization, selling, and consumer education to junior and senior boys in a residential school for the blind. In return, he would study braille, typing, and woodworking. From September to June, Bill would be at school except for vacations and an occasional weekend. The plan we had been working out with Mary came into being just then, and the year that Bill was away in his twin role of teacher-student was the year that Mary came to make her home with us.

I missed Bill. My hands seemed empty when he first went away, and the house was lonely without his cheerful voice and ready laughter. But when he came home, first for a weekend, then for the longer Christmas vacation, it was easily evident what the experience was doing for him. Talking about business put him back in the world that had been his for so long; being with blind people gave him ways and skills that might have taken him years to develop otherwise.

We had been taking whatever steps we could along the way, pushing wide whatever door opened a crack. Before another school year started, a new opportunity was presented to Bill. A private state-wide agency for the blind was ready for an executive director and Bill was asked to build a staff and develop a program. Acceptance would necessitate having an assistant with the various duties, including secretarial and driving. Bill was happier than he had been in three years. One event after another had been working out so beautifully, we felt sure that whatever was needed to complete the picture would follow the same pattern. Bill put an ad in a metropolitan paper stating his condition, his needs, and the work that would be entailed. Then he confidently waited for replies.

During the next two weeks seven letters came in answer to the ad, one from a city three hundred miles distant. In it, the writer answered thoughtfully and imaginatively every point that Bill had brought up. The whole was underscored by the assurance that the work, involving as it did social and personal service to the handicapped, was something to which he could gladly give his whole heart.

Bill answered Frank Hodge's letter immediately and asked him to come for an interview. It was the beginning of a long and happy relationship for them both.

Everything was fitting into place, and everything was proving its use. Adjoining the barn was a capacious carriage shed which we had used for storing cordwood. With the help of the carpenters who had done such sturdy work on the house, this had been made over into a little place for Mary to have as her own. Facing it across the barnyard was a small building which had once been a dairy; in it we had kept garden tools. Now, with the addition of a floor, some windows and an oil heater, this became an office for Bill from which he and Frank could carry on their work.

Shieling had expanded within itself to embrace work and fun, friends and helpers.

"Shieling is a family," Mary said.

It was a motif repeated often, sometimes applying to the humans and the life of the place, sometimes to the creatures who shared that life. Bonnibel had it her way when the mail, one morning, contained an invitation from the regional Scottish Terrier Club to enter her in their Members' Match.

"Do you suppose she would like it?"

"Up to a point," Bill said. "But it would be good for her, and it would be nice for us to see how she stands up among other Scotties."

Bill groomed her daily in preparation for the show and I exercised her in circles on the lawn. The grooming she relished, the careful walking bored her.

Sunday afternoon, when we arrived at the Show and took our seats with the exhibitors in the front row, I was a bit alarmed by the number and impressiveness of the assembled Scotties. Bonnibel was not. She barked a series of greetings that set off a chorus. From pointed ears to tail tip, she quivered with excitement.

"Oh Bill, what shall I do?" I whispered anxiously.

"Be yourself," he said comfortingly, "and you can certainly trust Bonnibel to be herself."

Bonnibel won one class after another—Green, Novice, American-Bred. Three times we walked back to Bill to put the ribbons in his hands. He reached down to stroke Bonnibel and she gave him one of her quick kisses, then tugged at the lead to get back into the ring.

Taking firsts in the preliminary classes qualified her for the finals, one of which was Best Female in Show. The prize was a small silver dish. When I proudly placed it in Bill's lap Bonnibel sat down beside him and pressed herself against his legs. The last class was called: Best Dog in Show.

"Come on, Bon."

Her ears went back. She had no intention of leaving Bill.

I pulled on her lead.

She looked at me as if I had insulted her, then turned back to Bill and ran her tongue quickly over the back of his hand.

"Bill, *say* something to her. Do *something*. Make her get up."

He laid his hand on her and spoke her name.

Bonnibel got up reluctantly and walked beside me into the ring. She wore her ears back and her tail looked like a piece of limp string. We took the place that had been kept for us.

"Handlers, walk your dogs," the judge said.

Bonnibel would not budge.

No words, endearing or threatening, no tidbit hastily drawn from my pocket and held under her nose, had any effect on her. The other dogs walked by us, smartly, self-consciously. I looked helplessly at the judge. His lips shaped the word "Dismissed."

"Come." I gave the lead a sharp pull and left the ring.

Bonnibel's ears went up. Her tail rose. She walked briskly with me back to Bill. I sat down beside him and we watched another Scottie get the trophy which ours might have had.

"Now what do you make of that!" I exclaimed.

"She knew she was the best dog in the show," Bill said. "It just bored her to have to prove it."

Generally willing to conform to reasonable procedure, Bonnibel did it only if it suited her convenience. Of the friends who came to the house, she had a particular affection for men. The low tones of a man's voice, the firm feel of his hands were to her liking. Certain things she did not like—among them flashlights, nail files, the moving of furniture, and wind of any origin. A sneeze was not an explosive sound; it was an insult. Bonnibel would look painfully at the perpetrator and leave the room. She could always maintain her dignity except in the presence of a vacuum cleaner. When it appeared she made her exit, and not merely out of the room but to the farthest bed in the house under which she could crawl.

It was against her principles to waste motion or energy and she never appeared in the kitchen for her supper until she knew it was ready; but she would leap to attention at the slightest hint of a walk or at a chipmunk's sassy challenge. She had an extraordinary sensitivity to fire. Once, when a spark jumped from the living-room fire and started smouldering in a rug, Bonnibel stood by barking furiously until she brought me to the scene. In an emergency, she could be relied on to put the well-being of her household above everything. We suspected that she had second sight. On more than one occasion we had come into a room and found Bonnibel facing an empty chair and barking conversationally with an occupant visible only to her.

Soon after the Members' Match we received a letter from the owner of a leading Scottish Terrier kennel, Ian MacDougal. He wanted to breed one of his champions to Bonnibel and have the choice of the litter. We decided to accept his offer.

Bonnibel appeared to level some very dour looks at us from under her long eyebrows the day we left her at the kennels, but when we called for her a week later Ian Mac-Dougal said with a sly smile, "I think you'll have some verra nice pups." And during the drive home Bonnibel, on the back seat of the car, had the air of being a superior person.

Summer days went on. The garden grew and so did Bonnibel. Walks tempted her less. She developed a fondness for secret places—a cool depression dug near the lilacs, a hole under the barn from which she emerged covered with dust and hayseeds.

Under MacDougal specifications a box was built for her to have her puppies in, but she would have nothing to do with it. Bill crawled into it, luring her after him. Under the soothing touch of his hands as he brushed her she relaxed and went sound asleep, but as soon as he left the box she did too. We placed her dinner in the box but she refused to eat it until it was removed. We put her special pillow in, but nothing would induce her to accept the box as a home for her prospective family.

The due time approached, the last day in August if our calculations were correct. During the afternoon, Bonnibel tried in every way she could to get over to the barn so she could retreat underneath it. She looked disdainfully at her supper and walked slowly into the guest room where the despised box had been placed. We lit the fire as the first cool wind of autumn was blowing over the countryside and the temperature had begun to drop.

Bonnibel sat down on her pillow outside her box as if she were waiting for her Appointment with Time.

"It's going to be much colder by morning," Bill said. "I

think I'll get a big log for the fire, one that will slumber through the night." He started across the lawn, his feet finding their way on the granite stones that linked house to barn.

Behind the barn northern lights were quivering, making the sky look as if moonrise were at hand. The Ancients would call that an omen, I thought. Well, so do I. To have the Aurora Borealis attend a multiple birth must signify something.

While I was standing by the door, waiting to open it for Bill, Dan drove by in his truck. He saw me and stopped to wave, then he caught sight of Bill coming from the barn with a huge log on his shoulder.

"Going to have a full house this weekend?" Dan shouted.

"It looks that way," Bill called back to him.

"Well, it kind of helps life along to have the house full now and then."

"Will it freeze tonight, Dan?" I asked.

He shook his head and waved good-by. "Nothing to worry about."

"How can he always be so sure about the weather!" I exclaimed to Bill. "He never listens to a forecast and I've not known him ever to be wrong."

"Well, I imagine that it's just sense," Bill said. "The thing a horse has, or a dog, only this time it's a man."

We went in the house, in to the room with the stencil designs on its walls. Bill set the chunk of maple carefully on the fire, tucking it well back.

"Full house, I wonder," he said quietly as he knelt down beside Bonnibel and ran his hands gently over her body.

After Bill went upstairs to bed, Mary and I stayed on in the guest room. It was warm, and seemed to be filled with content. The log slumbered on the hearth. Bonnibel slept peacefully, breathing deeply. We decided to get some sleep for ourselves and stretched out on the twin beds.

It was after midnight when I wakened suddenly. Bonnibel had crossed the room and was lying near my bed. Something like an unwilling sigh escaped her stoic self. I put my hand down and could feel her body contracting slowly, rhythmically. She left me and darted across the room into her box, making a small commotion among the newspapers with which its floor was covered.

By the time I could put a light on and get to her, I heard the sound of licking—furious, swift licking, then there was the tiniest of cries.

"Mary, come quickly!"

Peering into the box, we saw a small black object lying amid the tumbled papers. Bonnibel darted out to her pillow. Mary went to call Bill. By the time he got downstairs another puppy had arrived. Bonnibel was licking it as if life, which it did just then, depended on the motions of her tongue.

Bill sat cross-legged close to the fire and took the first-born, who had been temporarily abandoned, in his hands, cupping them for warmth over the tiny limp form. As soon as the secondborn uttered a cry, Bonnibel abandoned it and Mary took it in her hands. The pups were males and they were blissfully asleep, unaware that they had left one world for another. Eyes and ears were tightly sealed; small domed heads gleamed in the firelight.

Bonnibel walked restlessly around the room. Her sides were heaving. She was panting, and had no interest at all in her puppies. She wanted to go out, but we felt we could not let her just then. We three sat on the floor by the fire. The pups went on dreaming their only slightly interrupted dream. The clock struck four. Gray light of early dawn began to fill the room. Mary placed her pup beside the other in Bill's hands and went out to the kitchen to make some coffee.

"Aren't you stiff?" I whispered, forgetting that the sleeping mites could hear no more than they could see. "You've sat so long in that position."

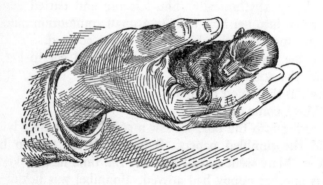

"I don't want to disturb the Little Boys."

Bonnibel wandered out to the hall. A sound came from her. It was sharp and high-pitched, more in surprise than pain. I went to her and saw that she was busily licking a third puppy. As soon as it cried she was satisfied and stopped licking, then she sauntered back to her pillow and lay down on her side, exhausted and relaxed. I picked up the third puppy. It was almost as big as the two males together.

"This one is an Amazon!" I placed it in Bill's hands for him to warm and took the others to tuck against the now-sleeping Bonnibel. Mary came in with the tray of coffee.

"There's something very special about that one," Mary said as she watched Bill fondling the pup. Then, after a few moments she took the little Amazon in her own hands, studied her carefully, held her up to her cheek, then laid her against Bonnibel. "Watch her," Mary said, "she knows how to do everything! I told you she was special."

The tiny paws reached instinctively as the mouth fitted itself around one of the full teats. Bonnibel opened one eye and looked at the three, then she went back to sleep while the puppies sucked on, drawing her milk into their bodies.

To feed, to sleep: that was the puppies' pattern of life, and for the first few days all that was required of us was a measure of watchfulness to make sure that they fed equally and that an even temperature was maintained in the room. Bonnibel was a dutiful mother. She spent hours lying quietly while the puppies fed or crawled around her. She cuddled them in her undemonstrative way, and she washed them constantly.

By the time they were three days old we knew them as distinct personalities: Jimminy was something of a clown, Cricket had a twist in his tail, Belinda was the blackest with five white hairs under her chin. Their smooth coats shone. They grew almost as we gazed at them. Their noses were cold. Their nails were like tiny wires. Their pads were soft as down. Their tails were almost as long as their bodies. Whatever they did—eat, sleep, crawl, whimper— they did it vigorously.

When they were a week old, Bonnibel gave us warning that she was a mother by sufferance, not by choice, and that she preferred our company to that of her children. She began to leave them frequently and for lengthening periods, so we put a hot-water bottle in the box and the puppies slept on it. Every two hours or so, Bonnibel returned to the box and barked sharply, then she went in, lay down, and let the puppies clamber around her, snuffling until they found her teats. If they cried plaintively when they lost themselves under her long nose or on her far side, she would nuzzle them into position. They sucked greedily, kneading her body with their paws to keep the milk flowing. When they had had their fill, they fell instantly asleep, mustaches white and milky.

At two weeks, they were sleek, fat, and sturdy. They could yawn, growl, and give muffled barks that sounded like bronchitis. Jimminy and Cricket did everything together. Belinda did everything in her own way. Either Mary or I described them to Bill.

"Their eyes are beginning to open," I said, on the morning of their two weeks' birthday. "Not wide yet, just a slit, but each one has a gleam of light in it."

"Can they see anything yet?"

"Oh no, but it's odd, that little slit makes me feel as if I could see them."

In another few days Belinda had her legs under her and could walk instead of crawl. Her eyes and ears were definitely functioning. Her back teeth had appeared. She carried her tail high when she went for a wander around the paper that had been placed outside the box. Jimminy and Cricket were often demanding, often bewildered, but Belinda was always adaptable. If she rolled over on her back after a meal and was too full to right herself, she decided that her back was where she wanted to be and stayed there. She loved the comfort of corners and would wedge herself into them, and the comfort of companionship. When her brothers were sleeping on the hot-water bottle, she would push herself between them and have warmth on both sides as well as beneath her.

During the third week, Bonnibel's milk supply began to diminish. The puppies were given their first taste of other food. Belinda lapped it sensibly, but the boys were furious. Wanting nothing but mother, they wailed miserably until even Bonnibel took pity on them.

Bill could invariably get them to eat when every ruse either Mary or I had employed failed. Sitting down on the floor, he would make intriguing sounds and move his finger slowly in the dish of pablum. Gradually curiosity, and with it appetite, was aroused. It was a long process, but Bill took the time to give himself to it. And the pups responded. After the pablum days were over, he lured them into eating chopped meat and vegetables. He even persuaded them that cod-liver oil was good. They were sure that it was if it had the taste of his finger, too. He helped them to eat properly, not bolting their food or stealing from one another. The puppies even began to develop some manners by the second month of their lives when their coats started to thicken and get tough.

The fingers that had made food edible proved capable of comfort when a small body was wracked by inner distress.

"Don't worry," Bill said to me confidently one day when I was sure that Cricket was not long for this world, "I'll just hold him for a while and talk to him. He's probably got a little too much Persian rug in him just now for comfort."

I left them together. When I returned, Cricket was sleeping peacefully in Bill's cupped hands, and I could only assume that the digestive process was going on normally.

There was discipline in those fingers, too, and understanding back of it.

"Jimminy didn't know it was your favorite dish towel," Bill said one day after a series of misdemeanors made me wonder if the pups would ever become civilized. "And as for that letter of Mary's—she shouldn't have left it on the floor. It was just paper to Cricket, and you know what the pups have been trained to do with paper."

"But Bill, have you really reprimanded them?"

"I have—" he paused, "spoken to them severely."

On a sunny October day when we were sitting on the lawn, alternately playing with the pups and watching them at their own games, Mary said, "Honestly, Bill, we never could have brought that family up without you."

"You might give their mother a little credit."

"She's so rough with them, Bill," I said.

"Well, she probably knows what they need."

"Look at them now—" Bonnibel was running across the grass while the pups pulled at her whiskers or any part of her they could catch. Then Jimminy saw a leaf blowing and raced after it. Belinda caught sight of a stick and dared anyone to dispute her right to it. Cricket challenged his brother to a wrestling match. Bonnibel sat down and panted, her long red tongue a tempting mark. One after another the pups threw themselves against her and the whole lot rolled across the green grass.

"It's like the worst kind of football scrimmage."

After their game the pups rushed to drink water, lapping it furiously. I had to take the bowl from them or they would have had more than was good for them. Jimminy looked at me reproachfully, one ear up and the other down. Cricket barked in protest. Belinda merely walked away.

"See how sensible she is!" Mary exclaimed proudly.

Of the three pups, Belinda's ears were the first to stand up. They looked huge, but they made her appear very smart. I realized what a handsome dog she was and described her all over again to Bill. Soon she would be losing her needle-sharp baby teeth.

"They're real little dogs now," I said, proud as Bonnibel was of her family.

"I expect it's time we asked Ian MacDougal to come over and have a look at them," Bill commented.

"Oh, no—" Then I remembered that raising the pups had been a business venture. It had never been intended that they should remain with us as members of the family, no matter how endearing they might be. I watched them racing over the grass again. Belinda could outrun her brothers, but Cricket could outwit both brother and sister. They found something to bark at and real sounds came from them. They barked on and on until Bill whistled to them, then all three came pelting across the lawn to hurl themselves into his lap.

Belinda, whom we had first called The Amazon, had come into the world with the gift of acceptance. From the hour of her birth, through the heyday of play, she was always willing to adapt herself to what must be. Stoically,

of course, that was part of her Highland nature, but gracefully too.

"I hope Mr. MacDougal won't choose Belinda," I said.

"Oh, I hope not, too," Bill agreed, "for Mary is so fond
of her."

When Ian MacDougal came to see the pups, they
greeted him with noisy joy. While he stood talking to us,
Cricket deftly untied both his shoelaces.

"That wee dog is going far-r-r," Mr. MacDougal said
as he retied his laces. He had his eyes on Jimminy. "That
one will be a champion before he's a year old, mark my
word."

"What about the female?" I asked anxiously.

"We-el, she's a bit on the big side, but that's no harm
for you."

I could not catch Bill's eye to signal my relief, so I
pressed his hand quickly. He smiled and nodded.

We sat on the porch with Bonnibel beside us while the
pups played their endless games, throwing themselves
down to pant for a moment, tumbling up again to race,
wrestle, or drag a stick around.

"They're r-r-real Scots," Ian MacDougal said.

Something about the pups must have stirred him
deeply for he began to talk about the ideal dog. That
meant a Scottish Terrier. As far as he was concerned, no
other breed existed.

"Ah, a Scottie is a gentleman, if the Lord ever made
one." Aware of Bonnibel, he dropped his hand to her
head. "And a lady, too. Honorable, independent, loyal.
Did you ever see one complain? They take life as it's given
them, and they've got far more sense than most humans."

"They're stubborn when they want to be," I said.

"What you call stubborn, I'd call fir-r-rm. True to
friends and down with all varmints! That's the spirit.

Your Scot will attack anything if his rights are at stake. He may die, that's no matter to him, but he'll never run away." He gazed across the lawn at the pups. "Any one of them would go down a fox hole and know what to do. They'll know as well what to do in a show ring." He turned to Bill. "I've made my choice, and I'm ready to make you an offer as well."

I decided that was a good time for me to go in and get the tea. When I returned, both men looked pleased. Bill had a slip of paper in his hands.

"Mr. MacDougal wants to take Jimminy as his part of the deal," Bill said to me, "and he'd also like to buy Cricket. He thinks both of them have real futures. Would you feel all right about that arrangement?"

"Why, yes—" It was not an easy word to say, but the boys had their own lives to live in the world and we would have their sister. "Yes, Bill, I think that is a very good arrangement."

Bill took out his wallet and slid the piece of paper in.

Ian MacDougal was talking now about his own Scotties. "See how the eyes flash in that wee one you call Cricket? And that's only a spark of the fire in his heart. Look at Jimminy! That's the braw spirit, and what a body it's housed in!"

He sipped his tea, ate some of his scone, then looked at me. "I've not had such a scone since I was last in Aberdeen."

"A Scottish friend showed me how to make them years ago."

"Tea and scones and a kippered herring," he murmured reminiscently. "That's a meal fit for a laird."

"The pups like kippers."

"Do they now? And haven't I been telling you they're real Scots?"

"We gave them kippers once to tease their appetites, and they've had them as an occasional treat ever since."

"You've not had trouble with their eating?"

"Oh no, they polish their plates and clean each other's whiskers."

"Aye, that's a Scot. They'll eat even when they don't feel up to it. It's as if they knew it was a duty to keep themselves str-r-rong."

An hour later, as we walked toward the gate, I never knew quite what happened. Ian MacDougal called to Jimminy and Cricket. They went to him expectantly. He picked them up in his arms, pushed open the picket gate and set the pups on the front seat of his car. They looked wholly his now, and ready for adventure. Belinda, puzzled at the separation, thrust her nose through the gate, then turned away and came over to stand beside us. Ian MacDougal drove off. The pups in the seat beside him had no eyes for anything but the road ahead.

The house seemed empty and unusually quiet, but Bonnibel slept on her pillow that night with a relaxation that must have been two-parts satisfaction. She had given to the world a family to be proud of, and she had given to them her best: indulging the puppies as infants, disciplining them when they were old enough to take it, helping them in every way to develop confidence.

When Bill showed me the check I gasped, "A hundred and fifty dollars for Cricket! How could he be worth so much?"

"You always said they were good pups."

"Yes, but hardly *that* good! Why, I would never have let Bonnibel be so rough with them if I'd thought—"

"It's the way they've been brought up that has brought out some of their rugged characteristics."

"May be so." But still I marveled.

Bill endorsed the check and I took it to the bank the next day.

Belinda became, what we suspect she always wanted to be, a home girl. Her name was soon shortened to Linda and her relationship with Mary was unquestioned. Bonnibel did not yield any authority to her daughter, but she equipped her to assume it in good time. News came, now and then, of the boys. Jimminy had fulfilled expectations and become a champion before he was a year old. Now he was siring a line of worthy progeny. Cricket had gone to Florida. Smaller than his brother, he developed more slowly; but by the time he was three, he had become a champion and was doing his part to raise the Scottish Terrier standard in the south. Bonnibel had a sudden illness. She bore it without a whimper and with characteristic dignity, but she no longer had her youth to help her battle it. Quietly the door closed on her rich complement of years and Linda became head dog.

A letter from Ian MacDougal asked if we would consider breeding our female, he again to have the pick of the litter.

Bill was out of town with Frank on one of the many trips made in the course of his work when Linda's puppies were born. When he returned, we introduced him proudly to the two new members of the household: Robin and Tammas, three days old. Robin was always stronger and took the lead over Tammas, but Linda kept them both in their places. She gave them more than birth and milk and early care; she imparted to them the feeling that the world was a wonderful place in which to be. Bones grew sturdy, coats shaggy, while confidence in themselves grew too. Whether they cut their teeth on table leg, knucklebone, or friendly hand, it was evident that they had teeth.

Stockily built, with the best traditional points, Tammas had the makings of a champion. His heart was warm, but a fiery spirit gleamed from his eyes. When he was four months old he was taken over by Ian MacDougal. Soon after, and three days before Christmas, an acquaintance of ours telephoned asking if we would sell Robin to her. She reminded us that the town clerk had recently lost the old dog who had been his constant companion for years, and she wanted to give him a new one as a Christmas present. Robin, like his mother, had been gifted with an affectionate, adaptable nature. This seemed the perfect answer for his life. That night I gave him a bath and an extra good supper. Bill spent a long time brushing his coat. He looked "braw" indeed, as Ian MacDougal would have said.

His donor arrived the next morning with a red ribbon which was soon tied in a bow on Robin's collar. Then we all went down to the town house to watch the presentation. The clerk sat behind his desk that was always piled high with papers. Robin, looking self-conscious, was held in the arms of his purchaser. She stepped toward the desk, ready to make a speech prepared for the occasion.

But there was something about that particular present that wouldn't stay wrapped in arms that were only temporary. Robin reached his nose forward to sniff the town clerk's face, then he began licking it. In another moment he had freed himself from one pair of arms and settled into another. There was no time for speechmaking. There was no need. Whatever should be said, Robin could say himself.

Bill telephoned the town clerk on Christmas night to see if Robin was behaving himself.

"Better than that," came the reply, "and say, does that dog like turkey!"

We heard of him often and saw him occasionally. He soon established his own procedures. Liking TV, he barked to have it turned on when he was the only person in the town clerk's sitting room. Civil weddings suited his Highland nature, and he never missed standing like an attendant beside the bride and groom. His master, in his capacity as Justice of the Peace, often had to pronounce sentence on lawbreakers. At such times, Robin remained under the desk.

We began to talk about having another dog.

"Not too big a dog," Bill said, "but it would be nice to drop my hand to a dog's head instead of having to reach for it around my ankles."

The more we talked about dogs, the more Shelties appealed to us. They stood knee-high, were rugged and responsive, and would be in something of the same tradition that we had had for so long. We wrote to a Sheltie kennel and got a book from the library to read more about the little collie from the Shetland Isles, and then we purchased a three-months-old pup. The day I brought him home from the kennel, Bill and Mary were sitting on the lawn in the warm May sunshine waiting for us. Linda was nowhere to be seen.

The little fellow was well born and well connected and he handled himself with dignity. He had sat beside me on the front seat of the car with an air of My-mother-told-me-to-be-brave-and-so-I-must-be; but he kept his distance from me. During the drive, our relationship was a formal one. When I lifted him from the car and set him down on the grass, shyness overcame his dignity.

Ears drooped, tail went between legs. He was uncertain of himself, unsure of us, uneasy about the fearful bigness of the world after the fenced security of his kennel. A series of shivers ran over him. Then Bill gave a low warbling whistle. The puppy listened for a moment. When the whistling sounded again he had not the slightest doubt but that it was for him. A degree of dignity returned, and with it courage. The Sheltie went slowly across the grass to the man who was waiting for him.

Mary and I held our breaths as we watched.

A moist nose sniffed. A gentle hand caressed. Pockets were explored and found to contain something good to eat. Gradually the limp tail began to move, the ears lost their wilted look. Suddenly the puppy began covering Bill's face with kisses as if he could not show his feelings quickly enough. He had found the one to whom he belonged. Then, quite as suddenly, as if exhausted by the discovery he had made, he sat down and leaned against Bill.

Mary started to describe him. White chest and white legs. Golden coat with a few dark hairs on either shoulder. Tail with dark shading down it and small white tip. Sturdy build, even though he was only a hint of what he would be. Fine head, long nose, even white markings. Warm, brown, almond-shaped eyes. "And, he has little golden eyelashes!"

"What shall we call him, Bill?"

Bill ran his hands over the golden-brown coat. The Sheltie lifted his black-tipped nose and kissed him quickly, furtively, as if it was something just between the two of them.

"Let's call him Tawn," Bill said.

And Tawn he was.

Linda ignored the newcomer for three days. Tawn made overtures to her and she turned her head away. Gaining confidence, he barked around her joyously, pleading for a game; but she would have none of him. The first night he had a wave of homesickness and whimpered mournfully.

It meant nothing to Linda. She paid no attention to him. Tawn learned to keep his distance and treat her with respect. Then Linda acknowledged his presence. She sniffed him all over; she began to play with him. Soon she was protecting him as if he were her own. She taught him all that a young dog should know. He became her dear friend; no less dear after he attained his growth and towered above her.

Tawn grew more golden as the summer advanced. He had much to learn, some of which Linda could be trusted to teach him, some for which we took responsibility. As a shy, sensitive animal he had much to overcome; all of which was not done his first year. But the best of his heritage came out as he grew, and it met our high hopes for him.

The stormy climate and rocky terrain of the Shetland Islands had given his forebears strength and stamina. Coming from a long line of work dogs, Tawn had a willingness to obey, particularly his master. He would leave anything he was doing to answer Bill's whistle, the low-pitched warble which had first spoken to him. He had a natural instinct to guard his property—Bill first, then Linda, the hens, the place in general. On the moors with his shepherd and sheep, Tawn's watchdog tendencies would have been commendable. We had to try to convince him that in New England, in the twentieth century, not everything and everyone were suspect.

Walking with him in the fields, his grace of movement was a lovely thing. "He's like a leaf, Bill, an autumn leaf —light, swift, airy in motion!"

Tawn turned and raced back to us, aware that he had been too long away from the one he loved and for whom he felt responsible. Ears back, tail streaming in the wind, he covered the distance to Bill, then jumped against him, reporting with his whole body.

Natural devotion matched with canny intuition made him immensely companionable. When Bill was alone—listening to his Talking Book, or to music, or rumi-knit-ting—Tawn would be with him, curled at his feet, restful yet always alert.

Tawn, full-grown, was big for a Sheltie. When standing, Bill could just reach the raised head if he dropped his hand to it. Tawn's color deepened. His white ruff stood out handsomely, his pantaloons were full, his tail conversational. Buoyant and gay with us, he was reserved with others and suspicious of strangers. Generations of train-ing, as well as responsibility, had given him the ability to work things out in his own way. He seemed to know what was expected of him, and he grew to fulfill it: responding to Bill's call, accompanying him around the place, or lead-ing him over the woods' trails, and always with a proud protective air. Affection meant everything to him and he had a feeling for its significance, making sudden demon-strations of love when there was no apparent reason for them.

Tawn wanted to please us, Bill especially. There were times when he failed, or when we misunderstood his in-tent. There were times when discipline was his due. He accepted it manfully, and then could not wait to show us his love.

"I think," Bill said, when Tawn was a year old, "that I must have everything that is essential for the good life—home, wife, friends, work, and now Tawn."

SIX ⅼ *With Summer Come Surprises*

B I L L and Dan were talking about the fire that had started when the town dump got out of control and spread to a nearby barn. The town was proud of the fact that no great harm was done as the fire truck got to the scene so quickly.

"That new young preacher gave us a sermon about dumps, last Sunday," Dan laughed. "Now what do you think of that?"

"Well, I'm not really surprised. "Doesn't he preach some of his best sermons on the things that happen right here in town?"

"He does, at that. He even used the dial system coming to town as an example in a sermon."

"Dan, did that lightning-rod salesman get around to your place yesterday?"

"Can't say as he did."

"Maybe he spent too much time here. But what a sermon that would make!"

"Now how, in the name of glory, do you figure that out?"

"Well, I was thinking that there are some people, grounded in neighborliness and goodness, who seem to have their own built-in lightning rods. When the human atmosphere gets loaded and a bolt is looking around for some place to strike, they don't get hurt even if they are hit."

Dan grinned. "How come you never got to be a preacher?"

Bill shrugged his shoulders and laughed, "Oh, that's not my line."

"What did you say was that salesman's name?"

"I've got his card somewhere." Bill's hands went through his pockets, then he called to me. "Wherever did I put that card the salesman gave me yesterday?"

"Where you put all your important reminders—clipped to your front pocket."

Bill reached up to the top pocket of his coat and drew the card from its clip. Turning it so the name could be seen, he handed it to Dan.

Dan scrutinized it carefully, then he put it away in a pocket. "It just may be that I'll get in touch with him sometime. Thanks, Bill." He started toward his truck. "I've got to get along now—told a man I'd meet him at the grain store at ten o'clock and it must be near that now."

" 'By, Dan."

Before he drove away Dan called out to Bill, "Remember that water diviner I told you about? I'm going to bring him over to see you one of these days."

"Make it a Saturday, Dan, so I'll surely be home."

When the sound of Dan's truck died down the road I heard the town clock striking ten. "Bill, how does he do it! He doesn't wear a watch but he seems to know the hour and he's one of the few people who always has plenty of time."

"Well, I guess he's just well oriented."

"Wish I were." My watch had recently failed and I had been told that it would be six weeks before it would be repaired. My day had neat compartments into which the watch enabled me to apportion time. I wondered what I would do without it. "Bill, I'm absolutely lost without my watch."

"Maybe you could draw on some of the signs around you," he said.

And so I began to do.

The whistle from the mill in the South Village was audible at 7 A.M. and again at 4:30 P.M. There were train whistles that could be heard twice weekly and were especially clear when bad weather was imminent: the louder they sounded, the nearer was the bad weather. And noon, on every day but Sunday, was marked by a double blast from the firehouse in the town. A carillon rang from one of the churches thrice daily. Heavy summer foliage or an easterly wind muffled the sound, but it could always be heard, and it was a reminder that time even in passing could be gay.

There was a sundial in our garden and why it was I could not understand, but there seemed to be more time in the days that were measured by the sun's shadow.

"Bill, it says a quarter to four."

His finger went lightly to his watch. "That's what it is. Didn't you hear the hens calling for their scratch?"

The hens were as punctual as the sundial. We could walk through the barnyard in midmorning or early afternoon and the hens went about their own affairs—pecking at the earth, dust bathing, laying; they might coo a greeting, rustle their feathers, and they might not. But walk anywhere near them between 3:30 and 4 o'clock and they were loud in their demands.

I began to discover so many ways of telling time that a watch seemed unnecessary. In the morning hours, the flight of swallows in the air was full of busy intent; in the late afternoon their flight was sheer abandon to the ecstasy of being. In the garden, the four-o'clocks could be depended on to open late in the afternoon no matter how gray or cool the day might be. Two hours later, as the air changed and the first hint of evening came, the night-scented stock started to pour out its fragrance; faintly at first, then gradually flooding the air.

Lingering over our supper on the porch, we often waited for one particular sound.

"It's time for the brook," Bill said. "Listen."

Then it came—the sound of rushing, tumbling water, as if the gates in a small dam had been opened. None had been, but some subtle change in temperature had occurred and the warm air rising carried the sound of flowing water clear and full to us on the hill above. It was part of the pattern of the day, as was the calling of the whippoorwill and the melodic song of the hermit thrush.

There was no doubt about it, without an ever-present watch time could be told in a larger way. It was a way that served very well as long as there were no trains to catch or tightly fitting schedules to adhere to. I began to see why it was that Dan always had time enough and to spare.

Birthdays belonged to the pattern of time, but they were not so much reminders of passing years as occasions for family festivals. They were Special Days, set apart from all the others in the year. Mary's coming in early spring, Bill's in midsummer, and mine in deep winter were shining events, no matter what day of the week they fell on or how busy our lives might happen to be. A birthday, complete with cake and candles, was one's own day: for honoring, for rejoicing, and for dedication. As such, it was to be observed in some unusual way, and the birthday person had full right to be the recipient of some gift that represented long-held need or desire.

Mary and I were always needing things—clothes, books, equipment for various activities. But with Bill it was different. He was carving his life with such simple tools that often it seemed there was nothing he needed at all. For weeks before his birthday, Mary and I accepted the challenge and matched minds in planning a fitting celebration.

Presents for Bill invariably intrigued the imaginations of his friends. There was one who always made him a box of fudge; another gave him a record; one liked to send him a tie whose texture was definite and unmistakable; from another came a box of pine soap, fragrant as woods after rain. And books: the kind that were good for family reading aloud. With so many evidences of practical thoughtfulness, there often seemed to be little left for us to do.

"What are you giving Bill this year?" Mary asked as her knitting needles clicked and the sweater she was making for him neared completion.

"I don't know."

"But his birthday is only a week off!"

"True, but I haven't thought of anything yet. Except—"

"What?"

"Mary, I've been thinking for a long time that I would really like to give him some water."

"Water!" The clicking of needles ceased. "Whatever do you mean?"

"A little water of his own to swim in—to row a boat over—perhaps even to fish—"

"You mean a *lake?*"

"Well, not exactly a whole lake. Frontage on a lake might be a better way of putting it."

"Land *and* water." Mary resumed her knitting.

I watched her fingers. To make a sweater was such a reasonable, tangible thing. To produce a lake was sheer fantasy.

Bill loved to swim, and he was a strong swimmer. A box of medals won in early competitions had long reposed in his top bureau drawer along with his socks. Swimming was the one activity that he could freely enjoy. Occasionally during the summer we drove the hundred-odd miles to the ocean for a swim in salt water; occasionally we had a chance to swim in one of the many lakes that dotted our countryside. We had dreamed once of having a piece of land on a lake, but it had been set aside along with other dreams. And now, here I was thinking of it again! The mere idea not only teased my mind, it tingled through me as a possibility.

"It seems preposterous," I said.

"It just may be reasonable," Mary replied.

That afternoon I went in to town to talk with the real estate agent. He listened carefully as I told him what I wanted. To my surprise he did not shake his head but turned to a file of properties headed FOR SALE. Moving quickly through them, he hesitated at one, went on, then stopped at another.

"This might interest you," he began cautiously, "but it's small. Three hundred feet on the shore line and about three acres in extent. It's pretty much in the woods."

"How far away is it?"

He looked up at the large-scale county map on his wall. "Probably about nine miles, not more than ten, from your house." Then he shook his head. "There's no road in. It would be quite inaccessible."

"How much is it?"

He named the price. "The owner isn't asking much because of the fact that there is no road. It will cost quite a bit to bulldoze one through the woods."

"We don't want a road. We want water. When can we see it?"

"Most any time."

"Now?"

"My time is yours," he said, with a gallantry that was good business.

We drove back to the house for Mary. While she was getting ready to go with us, I told Bill that we would both be away for an hour or so.

"Don't ask me any questions, Bill, for I can't give you any answers."

He nodded. There was the hint of a smile on his face. It was the time of year—like Christmas—when the fact was known and accepted that questions were not to be asked.

We drove seven miles north to a neighboring village, went through it, and soon turned off the highway and on to a dirt road that led through woodland. After a mile or so the road ran for about a hundred yards along the edge of a lake. There was a small dam and the water spilling over it fed a brook which pursued its way through the woods. Near the dam was a sort of harbor, made of granite boulders, where a half-dozen rowboats were moored.

"This is it. The Pond."

Mary gasped. "But it's so big!"

"Forty-six acres. Technically, and in State terminology, still a pond. I'll see if I can borrow a boat from someone. We can't reach the property any other way."

The real estate man left us and went to a farmhouse across the road which appeared to be the only near evidence of human habitation.

Mary and I stood by the dam and looked around us. The water slipping over it was the only sound in the stillness, that and the light slapping of rowboats as the breeze nudged them. What we saw was a fairly round body of water rimmed by forest. Along the shore grew pine, hemlock and birch, maple and oak. The trees reached back and climbed the low line of hills that met the sky. At the opposite end of the pond there appeared to be an inlet where rushes grew. Above it was a small eminence which, we had been told, was called Thumb Mountain. From its slopes a brook fed by springs poured into the pond. Standing there, with our ears sharpened by silence, we could hear the faint far flowing of the brook.

What Mary saw beyond the immediate scene I do not

know; what I saw was the shape of long-held heart's desire. Then I looked more closely. My eyes searched the shore line. Nowhere, except at the marshy inlet, was it anything but rocks. Huge, granite boulders. Rounded, angular. Beautiful in their way, but not inviting. No wonder the pond was frequented by only a few fishermen. No wonder there was some of its shore line for sale.

The real estate man came back and stood beside us. He had a pair of oars in his hands.

I shook my head. "It's beautiful, but far too rocky."

"Yes, it is rocky," he agreed, "and the depth is sudden. In most places the shore shelves off quickly to twenty or thirty feet. But let me show you the place I have in mind for you." He went toward one of the boats and started fitting in the oars.

I looked at Mary. She was taking off her sneakers and rolling up her jeans. "Don't let's go, Mary. I know it won't do. Swimming would be impossible with that kind of shore."

"You can't come this far and not go a little farther," she said. "Get in the boat. I'll push off."

Unwillingly, because in a setting which seemed like realization I could not bear to be disappointed, I got in. We rowed silently over the rippling water.

"There's one other dwelling," the real estate man pointed across the lake to a clearing only just visible in a thick stand of pines. "Summer people."

I could see the corner of a log cabin, the line of its roof, a stone chimney with a curl of smoke coming from it.

"So round," Mary was saying, as her eyes followed the line of the lake.

"They say it must have been a volcano ages ago," the real estate man said. "That would account for its depth and the rocky rim. Actually it's not so round if you see it

from the air, but shaped something like a Christmas tree
—the base is the inlet over there, the tip is by the dam."

We were moving along the eastern shore toward the
southern end of the pond. The distance between the rowboat and the shore was narrowing. Now if I tossed a peb-
ble ever so lightly it would not splash on the water but
thud on land.

"This is where the three hundred feet start." Our gaze
was directed to a gray-green boulder that rose out of the
water. We rowed slowly past tall trees—beeches with pale
green leaves, a stand of wide-boled white birches, a ma-
jestic oak, hemlocks with low-sweeping branches.

"This is where the three hundred feet ends." The boat
idled just off-shore from an enormous smooth rock that
sloped gently down and into the water. "The total acreage
is almost rectangular, bounded by the water on the west,
a road on the eastern end, and a stone wall marks its south-
erly side."

The oars dipped and lifted just enough to hold the boat
near the rock.

I looked at Mary. "This is *It*, isn't it?"

She nodded.

Now I realized that it was what I had dreamed of and
hoped for and prayed to find. It was what I had seen in
my mind's eye for a long time, for seeing it in reality it
was exactly right. The sloping rock was what made it possible; the rock that, in a granite gesture, linked water and
land. I could see Bill sunning himself on it, diving from
it, returning to it after swimming.

"It's the only piece of property I have—"

"It's the only one—"

The oars dipped deeper. I could feel the boat turning,
but I could not take my eyes from the rock and the tall
trees rising behind it. Slowly we moved across the water;

slowly the rock merged into distance, but never disappeared. Somewhere hope and reality became one.

We said little to one another as we rowed back to the dam. The boat was tied up. The borrowed oars returned. We got into the car and headed for home.

"Would you like to come back to my office now?"

"I'd rather come in tomorrow."

"My time is yours."

Necessary details of business could wait. The magic moment stayed.

During the few days that remained before Bill's birthday, Mary and I explored the piece of land from the boundary at the road. We cut a trail through the woods and discovered that it was about a ten-minute walk from the stone wall at the crest of the hill where we could leave the car down to the water. It was a leafy, pine-strewn trail, mostly downhill. There was a silence and secretiveness about it; for many years the solitude under the great trees had not been broken save by the creatures of the forest. We cut away low-hanging branches and went around rocks, keeping the path as narrow as an animal trail. We did some clearing near the water's edge, not a great deal but enough so Bill's feet could find their way.

On the morning of his birthday a warm gentle rain was falling. It was needed, as rain in summer often is, and so it seemed a part of the day's benediction. We told Bill that we were going on a picnic after breakfast, whatever the weather might be. He always fell in agreeably with our surprises, and this was one time when his blindness aided our plans. When he came to the table, we sang "Happy Birthday" and the dogs barked gleefully as they sensed the unusual jollification. After Bill had sat down, we placed before him a token that Mary had made. In a wide bowl, an inch deep with water, she had put a smooth chunk of granite. Beside it, a three-inch high pine seedling was tucked into some moss. A tiny birchbark canoe floated on the water. Near the rock were twigs. Other smaller, rougher pieces of granite rimmed the water. It was the pond in miniature.

Bill felt the bowl, then its contents. We held our breaths as his fingers moved from one telltale piece to another. He started to smile.

"Is it—" and then he stopped. The smile froze on his face. His hands dropped to his lap. He would not say what he thought it might be in case it wasn't.

For years I had been haunted by a memory of a story out of Bill's childhood. When he was a boy of eight, a Westerner visiting his father had filled him with tales of the Great Plains—of cowboys and their horses, of small boys and their ponies. "As soon as I get back to the ranch I'll send you a pony. Would you like that?" Days passed. Then weeks. The eager boy watched and waited. Months passed. The pony never came. A man's memory was short, a boy's long enough to groove a lifetime. Bill had begun then to live only in the attainable. What he learned as a boy was to serve him well years later.

"Bill, it's true. Look at what's beside it. At the left."

Near Mary's miniature lake was a scroll. Bill found it, untied the ribbon around it and handed it to me. The smile melted. With his fingers he began again to explore the rock, caress the pine, push the canoe around the water.

I unrolled the scroll and read what I had written:

Know, O William, by this present, that a certain three hundred feet in length, and thrice that in depth, of land in our neighboring northerly township is to be deeded to you, your heirs and assigns, in perpetuity. This land is comprised of tall timber and granite rock, situated on a body of water called The Pond, ten miles from Shieling's door. It has full benison of the elements and lies well open to the sun. It is accessible by boat and secret trail, and is yours on this your natal day in warrant of the love borne you by your wife, Elizabeth. Necessary for the execution of this deed is your full and pleasured consent.

Signed, sealed, but not to be delivered until seen, in the presence of witnesses.

My name followed. It was witnessed by Mary. The dogs had put their pawprints near the daub of red sealing wax that made it official.

An hour later, with a picnic luncheon packed in the rucksack, bathing suits and towels in a waterproof bag, we were on our way to Bill's land.

Leaving the car at the stone wall, we followed the secret trail. The dogs shared our sense of wonder, for they went quietly through the woods and stood with us on the big gray rock lifting their noses to the stillness and finding in it no lure for hasty pursuit. The water was calm. The pines and birches, hemlocks and maples around the shore were dripping. The clouds were so low that even little Thumb Mountain was enveloped by them. Bill stood and breathed deeply. He bent down to feel the water, then smiled as if he would never pull his face straight again. Arm outstretched, he followed the outline of the pond as Mary described it minutely to him.

Then we were all overcome by silence.

When a dream that has been long held—nourished with hope but relinquished so often that its existence has seemed to be only in imagination—becomes tangible,

there simply are no words. Set aside but never abandoned:
perhaps that was the key to present reality.

After a while we went swimming. The dogs comforted
themselves in the shelter of a hemlock whose low branches
kept the ground dry. They looked at us pityingly then
curled up for sleep, Linda's long black head resting on
Tawn's golden rump. The water was warm. The fall of
the rain just enough to break the surface, not enough to
add sound to the stillness. There was nothing to guide
Bill—neither the feel of the sun nor a breeze to ripple the
water—but he needed no guide. Sometimes I called
"Right" when he was heading out too much, or "Left" if
he turned downstream. Sometimes just the patter of our

voices as Mary and I swam near the shore and talked together was enough.

Later joining the dogs in their green shelter, we had
our sandwiches, and tea hot from the thermos. Rain
dripped down from the hemlock needles. Rain dripped
down our noses. I had never seen Bill happier. Looking
back over the years to the day of our marriage when, his
face radiant and his eyes shining, he had turned to me and
said those words, whose wonder time was to teach, "My
wife,"—even then, he had not looked happier.

The Acre, as it was called that first day and as it
remained, became Bill's other home, the place where he
knew full freedom. His sneaker-shod feet, almost as sen-

sitive as his hands, could find their way over the trail from the stone wall to the water whether he had Tawn beside him or not. Near the shore, the trees were familiar to him, and the rocks. It was his world, a woodland world, remote, quiet, beautiful: a jewel set in timelessness.

When another year and another birthday came around, a small cabin was built a few feet in from the shore. Its one room held a fireplace with raised hearth, a table, some chairs, a folding cot, and the equipment needed for simple living. Bill often spent the night at the Acre, quite alone, not even with Tawn to companion him. The lapping of the water, the soughing of the wind gave him companionship. Birds hovered in the trees, chipmunks chittered from the stone wall, pounding hooves told of the near running of deer. Occasionally there were fishermen on the pond, drifting around patiently, intent on their own pursuits, calling a greeting or exchanging a few words with Bill, but never lingering long. Their interests were elsewhere and Bill was left to his happy solitude. A monk meditating in a desert retreat could not have been more alone; but Bill was never lonely.

When I returned in the morning to get breakfast, Bill had a dozen wonders to share with me out of his night. While lying in the hammock, he suspected that it was a raccoon who had scrambled down the tree at the hammock's head and run off into the woods. An owl had called across the lake over and over, "as if it were having singing lessons. And time," Bill said, "seemed to be marked not by hours but by fragrance. The dampness of the night air brought out deep rich odors. I knew when the dawn was coming for there was such freshness in the air, even before the first bird sang."

"But you did get some sleep, didn't you?" I asked anxiously.

"Oh yes, enough," he assured me.

"Don't you get lonely?" A friend asked once, shuddering at the thought of the woods at night. "Why, I'd be scared."

Bill looked as if he did not know the meaning of either word. To be alone at the Acre put him on the receiving end of Nature. So much came to him in the stillness that no night was ever long enough.

The Acre was a place where life was, as nearly as possible, reduced to elementals: simple shelter, primitive forces of fire and water. Light came, when needed, from a candle or a kerosene lamp. By virtue of what it was and had always been, the Acre imposed itself. Time moved slowly. Thoughts went deep and dared to soar, for nowhere was there any pressure to conformity. Around it brooded peace, pervasive as the hemlock shade and the lapping water. Modern living had a way of fragmenting life, spreading it so that it became thin. At the Acre, inner resources were called on, neglected powers revealed, and life assumed a sturdy wholeness. A few hours, or a day, spent there was enough for restoration. It was not an escape from daily life for any of us; it was renewal for daily life.

One morning, when I went over to join Bill for an early breakfast, he was neither in the cabin nor on the big rock. I did not want to call, for there was a sanctuary stillness to the woods and the hour. I went up to the High Place, a rise of land not far from the cabin. Bill was sitting there, as quiet as the pond below him in the windless morning light. His eyes were closed, his hands held a pine cone. He would have responded instantly if I had called, but there was no need to disturb him.

Returning to the cabin, I got life in the fire, put the coffeepot on the trivet, laid strips of bacon in the frying pan.

Breakfast would announce itself when it was ready. The last lines of a poem George MacDonald had written to a friend threatened with blindness were running through my mind—

> And when thou hast wearied thy wings of prayer,
> Then fold them, and drop gently to thy nest,
> Which is thy faith; and make thy people blest
> With what thou bringest from that ethereal height,
> Which whoso looks on thee will straightway share:
> He needs no eyes who is a shining light!

No, that was not wholly true, and no one could say that life was not better with sight; but it was only one of five senses.

When Bill appeared for breakfast, he was full of his adventures. "I had a caller last night," he said.

"Deer? Raccoon? Owl?"

"No, a fisherman. He was on his way back to the dam after what I judge had been a fruitless hour or two angling for horn pout. He called and asked me if I knew the time. I told him it was 9:17. He said I must be kidding and that he'd come near enough to the rock to flash his light on me so I could see my watch. I told him I didn't need the light and he said, 'Don't you know it's nearly dark?' "

"Oh Bill, what did you say then?"

"I said I didn't know."

One summer day, when Bill's birthday was again on the horizon, Mary said to me, "Water calls for a boat."

"Mmm," I agreed. "I know it does. A rowboat."

"Yes. That canoe was fine, but it wasn't the exactly right thing."

The previous autumn we had had the loan of a canoe for a month. It had given us great enjoyment—paddling up to the inlet in the long warm afternoons, paddling around the lake in the evening, but when the season was over we returned it willingly. A canoe was a magical thing, but for us a rowboat would be more practical.

Mary began making inquiries. We discovered to our surprise that rowboats—whether in stores or catalogues—were expensive things.

"You wouldn't think it would be so hard to find a small plain rowboat," she said, after she had followed a clue that led her to talk with a local fisherman, "but it is. There just aren't any boats around. There don't even seem to be any used ones available."

It was midsummer. Whatever boats might have been for sale in the spring had found owners.

"We've only got three more days," Mary said, "and we've exhausted every immediate possibility."

"What did your fisherman say?"

"That he'd sell me his boat in October."

"That won't do us much good now."

"So I told him."

The next day I had to be in the state capital, some forty miles north, so I went in to a sporting goods store and asked about rowboats.

The clerk was sorry that he couldn't help me. "A plain flat-bottomed, old-fashioned rowboat, you'd think we'd have them but we don't. Not this time of year. Everything seems to run into money these days." He called to another clerk. "Lady wants a rowboat. I told her we were out of stock until next spring. Know where she might pick up a second-hand one?"

Shaking his head sadly he came over to join us.

"New or second-hand," I repeated. "Wood not metal. Big enough for three people, but light enough so we can handle it ourselves."

He stopped shaking his head. "Seems to me I saw a

boat just like what you want sitting out on a fellow's lawn 'bout a mile east of the city line. He makes them in his spare time. That was a week ago. Maybe he's sold it by now."

He gave me the directions and I lost no time in following them. I knew I had found the place when I saw a rowboat sitting on a front lawn with a sign saying—

FOR SALE　$35

Mary and I could certainly afford that much for Bill.

It looked a nice job. Plain. Solid. All new wood painted gray. Small bow and stern seats, wide middle seat. I walked round and round it, hardly able to believe that it was real. Then the owner-maker appeared.

He was a fruit farmer and we spent a good deal of time talking about the strawberry crop that had been and the apple crop that was ripening. By the time we got around to talking about the boat I was convinced that the year was a good one for fruit.

"It's pretty late in the season for people to want boats. I'll throw in a pair of oars, too, if you're interested."

If I was interested!

I couldn't wait to get home to tell Mary about the boat and to plan with her how best it could be transported to the Acre. Bill had often said he could sense an electrical quality in the air when a family scheme was afoot. We tried to act calm and to give him no hint of our excitement.

On the morning of his birthday, Bill and I went to the Acre. Mary was a little vague about joining us in the afternoon. "Oh, I'll be over when I get some work attended to," she said airily.

"Surely for supper?" I reminded her.

"Oh, yes! Usual time?"

"Thereabouts."

I hoped we were not appearing too casual on this Day of days.

Bill and I swam, sunned ourselves on the rock, swam again, ate our picnic luncheon. We had just begun a double acrostic when I heard a long-awaited sound. At the dam, where the road ran close to the water, a truck rumbled to a stop.

"You know, Bill, I think I'll go and look for some blueberries. They'd be nice to have for our supper, don't you think?"

"Is Mary apt to come soon?"

"She should be here before too long. Perhaps I'll meet her."

"You'll have more berries if you do. Are you taking the dogs?"

"No. Stay, Tawn. Stay, Linda." My admonitory gesture was unnecessary. The warm summer day had filled them with drowsiness and they were lying in one of their black-and-gold patterns in cool shade near the water's edge.

"I won't be very long."

I picked up a bucket and, obeying what seemed a wholly irrational impulse, thrust my bathing suit and Mary's into it, then I went the shortest way through the woods to the dam. Mary had made arrangements with a friend who had a truck to drive her up to the fruit farmer's for the boat. The truck was driving off as I arrived and the boat looked more beautiful than when I had first seen it. On the shore, with its tip just touching the water, it was waiting to be launched. We were as proud of it as if our hands had made it.

"Does Bill suspect anything?"

"No. I told him I was going blueberrying."

We set the oars in the locks, put my bucket on one of

the seats, added our sneakers to its contents, then waded
in to push and drag the boat into the water. Then we
stood speechless: as if it were a giant sieve with invisible
holes, the boat quietly filled with water. Water was almost
up to the gunwales before we were able to say anything.
Then the keel settled down on the shallow bottom as comfortably as an old dog in his bed.

"It's dry," Mary said, "bone dry. It's been sitting on
that lawn for weeks in the hot sun. It will take days for
the wood to expand enough to fill the cracks. With everything we thought of, we never thought of that!"

"But we haven't got days—it's today we want Bill to
have the boat."

"We can't row it to the Acre, that's certain."

"Could we float it?"

Mary said no.

"Couldn't we bail it out, turn it over, and float it keel
up?"

"Dragging it by a rope from along the shore? I doubt
it."

"No, swimming it. You at one end, me at the other."

Mary looked at me. I looked at her. Bill would have
called it an electrical moment.

"How was it you brought our bathing suits?"

"Sheer hunch, nothing else."

We changed quickly in the woods, used the bucket to
bail the boat, turned the boat over—not without difficulty
—then placed the oars, and the bucket with our clothes
stuffed into it, on the keel. Wading beside the boat, we
pushed it until we could start swimming the quarter mile
to the Acre.

Everything traveled well. We had plenty to talk about
as we swam slowly along, one guiding, one pushing, alter-
nating now and then. We wondered how an airman, see-

ing us, might decipher our situation. As we drew near the Acre, we ceased talking and curtailed splashing.

Mary's white cap bobbed up beside me. "Have you thought of a name for the boat?" she whispered.

"I was just going to ask you that. Yes, I have. The Blueberry."

"Just what I was going to say!"

When we could see Bill's blue-jeaned, blue-shirted figure in the red hammock between the hemlocks, we started to sing—a birthday greeting to the tune of the "Volga Boat Song."

He sat up to listen, then he stood up. I could see him smile as he found his way among the familiar trees and came down to the water to greet us. We dragged the boat part way up on the rock and Bill brailled it from stem to stern, running his hands along the gunwales, the oars, the seats. Another dream had come true.

"It's yours, Bill, all yours."

"Just as everything over here is."

"What will you call it?"

"Didn't you say you were going blueberrying?" He looked at me, then at Mary. "Why not call it Blueberry?"

Like Tawn, like the Acre itself, Blueberry was one more dimension added to Bill's life. A friend soon equipped it with a rudder and Bill rowed vigorously, tirelessly, while one of us sitting in the stern steered effortlessly. We spent long warm days on the water, mild starry evenings. The dogs never seemed able to get enough boating. Linda sat in the bow, alert and interested. Tawn sat close to Bill, between his knees or curled up at his feet.

It was hard to wait for another year as the next present was so obviously necessary and so possible. A boat called for a dock as bread called for butter. Always there seemed to be people ready and able to help us with our plans.

When July came around, a local carpenter went over to the Acre to study the situation and agreed to build us a dock fifteen feet long and three feet wide. He made it in his shop, floated it over from the dam, and installed it the day before Bill's birthday.

Bill might have suspected something, but he always gave us our full due of surprise. When we went down to the rock on his birthday morning, all ready for a swim in the hot sunshine, we asked him to take just one more step.

"But that will be in to the water and I don't want to go in yet."

"Try it," we urged.

He did, and when his foot came down on sun-warmed wood, he smiled. "You've done it again!"

The dock was immensely practical. It gave a place to tie the boat to and it made getting in and out of the boat much easier. It was grand to dive from, to return to. It had many uses, but none of us realized until we experienced it the sheer delight it could give. It offered an extension over water into air. To lie stretched out on it, wet from a long swim with the sun slowly drying us, was to have water on three sides, air above, and to feel a curious detachment from the land. In the evening, to lie on it as the stars began to appear and the black line of trees from the opposite shore stretched, shadow-wise, longer and longer over the water, was to feel almost suspended in space.

"Now the bats have started to come," I said. Gazing up in to the darkening sky, I had become aware of the small-bodied creatures who were darting like swallows through the air, dipping to the water then wheeling treeward.

"What a tumbling flight they have," Bill murmured.

I watched them more closely. That was exactly it. They

were tumbling through the air with every appearance of carelessness, but able to change direction so adeptly that they never collided with anything or each other.

"That's it, Bill. That's really it. How did you know?"

"When you spoke of bats I saw them. I can remember their flight and the way they fling themselves around in the air."

Lying there as the dark came down, I could soon see nothing but the outline of trees, and even that became one with the darkness. But Bill went on seeing.

SEVEN ✦ *Each Day Its Own Reward*

DURING these intervening years the program of service
to the blind, which Bill had initiated, had expanded as
had the agency staff. Adequate headquarters had been established in a centrally located city about forty miles
north. Bill's week was divided between administrative
work, where his business experience proved invaluable,
and visiting blind people in their homes, where his own
blindness formed a common bond. Frank, who now lived
about a mile away from our house, gave himself as unspar-
ingly to the work as did Bill. He never let the long hours—
early starts and late homecomings—dim his zest for the
chosen work of service to others.

As Bill's week developed a pattern, so did my days. I
devoted morning hours to writing and afternoon hours to
care of the house, the garden, and some community activities. The satisfaction of published work began to be mine.

Bill's deepest satisfaction came in the realization of the new meaning that was quickening many lives. The objective, he felt, was not to remodel a blind person's life but to uncover and release frustrated desires and hopes. It was often difficult to persuade the blind person and his family to accept the limitations of blindness and to recognize the potentialities. And both were needed to achieve the eventual goal of self-help, self-care, and integration into the sighted community.

Many material aids and devices were available for the blind and often the introduction of a braille watch or clock, or even a self-threading needle and braille tape measure, would loosen an attitude made rigid by despair. Bill knew that idleness could corrode the spirit. To overcome this and provide a sense of independence and income, the agency had developed a home industry program. Equipment, training, and materials were provided, wages paid, and the well-made products were marketed through the agency's own craft shop and state-wide sales.

Fund raising and public education were two other important parts of the program. Bill took every opportunity to speak before service clubs, professional and church groups, and other organizations. In addition to describing the work of the agency, he would demonstrate many of the aids and devices, and explain to the audience how to be most helpful when with a blind person.

His work was not all serious and his sense of humor was always an asset. We looked forward to the weekends when we were all together again and Bill would tell us some of the highlights of his work during the week. Our circle of friends was constantly widening, but it was during the weekends now that we could make the most of it.

One Saturday morning Dan telephoned to ask if we were all at home. We assured him that we were and that we were ready for anything. He arrived a short while later with his water-divining friend whom he had long wanted Bill to know. Dan introduced us to Kester and we shook hands all around. I liked the way Kester's blue eyes twinkled under his white thatch of hair. I liked the firm grip of his hand. I was excited at what the little bundle of forked sticks under his arm might mean. Dan knew that we had been wanting to locate a spring of water in the woods near the old sugar house, and he felt that Kester could help us.

Mary called to the dogs and soon we started off in the direction of the woods. Bill rested his hand lightly on my arm as he did when we walked together, and the dogs ran circles of joy around us all at the prospect of a walk at such an unexpected time of day.

I knew that water diviners, or dowsers as they were often called, were extraordinarily gifted people who, by means of a forked stick, could locate water in the earth. Country people held them in great respect; city people were apt to scoff. I found myself eying Kester dubiously. I could be persuaded; I wondered if I would be.

Bill refused to comment. He would not even speculate, no matter how much Mary and I did. "Let's wait and see," was all that he would say.

Once at the sugar house, Dan and Bill leaned comfortably against the gray slab wall. Tawn stood close to Bill, reaching his muzzle up so Bill could rest a hand on his head. Mary and I sat down on the ground. I called Linda to me. Stroking her chest, I hoped to lure her into an oblivion that would counteract any scent of porcupine or squirrel that might tempt her to the chase.

Kester laid his Y-shaped sticks neatly on the ground. "Some use wands of willow, maple, or elm," he said, "and

I've used wands from apple, pear, and peach, but I like witch hazel best."

"Why did you bring so many?" I asked.

"They break, lady. The power can break them in two." He looked at me, but his blue eyes were not seeing me.

He stepped away from us with the two prongs of his wand clasped tightly, one in each hand and the point facing outward, parallel to the ground. He walked two or three paces in one direction, then turned and walked slowly in a line with the sugar house. His face was tense, his grip tight. I saw the veins stand out on his hands. Nothing existed for him then but his witch-hazel wand, freshly cut and full of sap, and somewhere underground a vein of water. As Kester walked over the pine needles and fallen leaves, his grip tightened. A line of sweat began to glisten along his brow.

"Bill," I whispered, "the point of the stick is going down—slowly, oh so slowly. There! It jerked suddenly. Just as if—"

"As if an unseen hand had come up from the earth and pulled it down," Mary said.

Kester walked back and forth to show the direction of the vein of water, then he stood still. He said nothing for a moment or two. He was like a person coming out of a trance. Then he looked at his wand. The bark had been loosened where his grip had held it tight. There were two gashes as if a knife had run down the bark and from them the damp yellow of naked wood looked out.

"There's water there, a good strong vein," Kester said. He did not move until Dan drove two or three sticks in to the ground to mark the course. "But I can't tell you how far down it is."

I took the stick from him. No doubting Thomas was ever more penitent. *"How* does it happen?"

"It's been happening since earliest times, lady, but no one's been able ever to say rightly how. All kinds of people have tried to explain it—scientists, geologists, psychologists, but nobody can. I don't try. I just let it work for me, and I've found a lot of water for a lot of people in my eighty-odd years."

"Will it do it for anyone?"

"They say the power runs in families, but it's only my youngest granddaughter has it in ours. I've an idea your man might have it."

Bill laughed. "I'd like to see."

"No time like this for trying." Kester picked up another of the forked sticks and placed it in Bill's hands, showing him how to hold it; then he walked behind Bill with his arms around him and his own hands also on the stick. They went slowly over the ground and when they crossed the vein that Kester had earlier discovered the point of the stick turned down so fast and the double grip was so firm that the stick broke.

"Here's another one," Kester said. "Now you try it for yourself. You can see why I always cut half a dozen wands before I go dowsing."

Bill, with his hands grasping the forked stick, walked carefully over the ground, over the known vein of water, back and forth, crossing it twice. Nothing happened. There was not even a quiver in hands or stick.

Kester smiled. "You never can tell with whom it will happen until you try."

Then we all tried in turn, but none of us had been given the gift.

Sitting down on a nearby stump, Kester took a clean white handkerchief out of his pocket and wiped his face. "I'm not so young as I once was."

"Rest a while," Bill urged. "It must take a lot from you to hold against that pull."

"And you have to hold against it to find the true vein," Kester explained. "When it gets to where you can't hold any more, then you've found it."

"Some say," Dan spoke slowly, "that there are magnetic elements in the soil and in the man, and when he passes over water a tremendous magnetic current draws the stick down."

"Could be," Kester murmured, though he did not appear to be paying much attention to Dan. "Some things you can't explain," Kester went on after a pause, then he folded his handkerchief neatly and put it away. "I've a notion that it's best to go along with them without trying to account for them." He got up slowly from the stump. "When I discovered that I had the gift, I figured it was something the good Lord had given me to use in His service."

We started walking back toward the house. At the bridge over the brook we stopped to rest for a few minutes. Dan reached down into the brook for some of the water cress that grew there. He handed a bit to each one of us which we ate. It was hot to the taste, but crisp and refreshing.

"How did you know you had the gift?" Bill asked.

"It happened more than seventy years ago when I was a boy—" Kester began, as he leaned against the rail of the bridge and looked down into the water flowing beneath us. The summer had been hot and dry. Wells had given out. Brooks were low. Kester and his brothers had been toting water for the cows from a lake a mile away. His father had begun to think he would have to butcher some of his herd because the pastures were getting so thin.

"I wanted to help," Kester continued, "and it was then

I remembered a story my grandfather had told us boys once about a water witch. The people were so scared at what had been done for them that they ran the witch out of town. But they had water. I cut myself a forked twig of witch hazel and went to a piece of pasture where no one could see me. I walked up and down, crossed and recrossed that land until my feet got tired and my arms ached and I knew it was past supper time, but I had to keep trying. Then it happened. The point of the stick was drawn down to the ground against everything I could do to keep it up, and a fourteen-year-old farm boy has a pretty good set of muscles.

"I tried it again and again. It happened every time when I walked over and along that particular spot. I knew it was a strong vein, and I was mighty scared at what had happened. I drove what was left of my stick into the ground, then I ran home yelling as if a bear had come out of the woods. Pa believed my story, but Ma was cross at me for being so late for supper."

"And did you find water?"

"Did we! Pa, my brothers, and I went out that night and dug by the light of the moon. Six or seven feet down beneath that dry cracked topsoil, we found the sweetest, purest, runningest vein, and it's never gone dry in all these years!"

Kester could have gone on with his stories, for his memory and enthusiasm seemed as unfailing as the springs of water he had released from the earth, but time was getting on. Dan had chores to do, and he had to take Kester home first.

"Let me know how deep you have to go," Kester called, as he waved heartily from the cab of Dan's truck.

We stood by the gate as they drove down the road.

"A rare gift indeed," Mary murmured.

As we walked back to the house, Bill said, "It's interesting about gifts, and there's something about handicaps that often uncover hidden skills. Frank and I ran into a case a week or two ago with a little different slant to it."

"Really, Bill?"

"You haven't told us that story yet."

"Well, it happened a few days ago. We had a call to make on an elderly woman who had recently lost her sight. She lived in the country with her retired husband and when we arrived she greeted us with a broad smile and said, 'Do you know that blindness can bring out talents you never knew existed before?' I was thrilled and urged her to tell us. 'Believe it or not,' she began, 'but there's never been better housecleaning, or mending, or even cooking in this place before.' Frank and I exclaimed at her rapid adjustment and began to compliment her. 'Oh, don't compliment me,' she laughed, 'my blindness has uncovered these talents in my husband!' "

Mary and I were often the beneficiaries of Bill's endless fund of stories. If we were involved in the kitchen with a meal that was not quite ready, we could always rely on Bill to keep our guests entertained.

"Mary, he's telling the dog story again—listen!" I stopped mashing the potatoes. Mary stirred the gravy noiselessly.

It was something that had happened when we were living in Paris several years ago. Bill had gone out one morning to get a paper. Seeing a little black dog running excitedly in the street, panting hard and apparently lost, Bill had whistled to it. The dog paid no attention but a taxi pulled up beside him and Bill had to explain in somewhat limited French that it was not a taxi but a dog he wanted. Finally he got hold of the dog. The address on its tag was that of a *Boucherie* a block or two down the

street. Bill went there and told the proprietor that his
little dog was running around in the midst of traffic. The
butcher smiled and pointed up the street saying, "Il n'est
pas perdu. Il a une fiancée, là."

Times without number I had heard the story, but I
could always laugh at it as at the first telling. Bill never
seemed to relate it any differently, but he was a natural-
born storyteller and listening to him one was invariably
caught up in a magic as soon as his voice took over.

"Do get on with mashing those potatoes," Mary whispered. "We'll never have dinner ready."

"All right." I started in at the potatoes again, then
I remembered something. "Mary, do you know that in the
Koran it says, 'He deserves Paradise who makes his com-
panions laugh.'"

One afternoon, on my way to town, I stopped to call on
an elderly friend. As I lifted my hand to place it on her
knocker, the door opened. She was as surprised to see
someone standing on her doorstep as I was to have the
door open before I had made a sound.

"Well now," she said, "and I was just going out to see a
face! I haven't seen one but my own all day and yours will
do. Come in and sit down."

The house was filled with the sweet-sharp smell of spice
and on the table in the kitchen was a row of jars, their contents amber in the slanting rays of the sun.

"I've been making some ripe cucumber pickle. One of
those jars is for you to take along home with you. I kind
of thought Bill would like it. What's new?"

Before I could rally my thoughts to relay some piece of
human interest, she was telling me of her own observa-
tions. The current story in town was of a young man who
was having "wife trouble." I had heard bits of it but had
not been able to patch together much of the story.

"You know something? I haven't got any sympathy for that young man. He tells his troubles to too many people. Troubles are things you should keep to yourself."

"Like skeletons?"

"Well, not quite that bad, but it seems to me they multiply every time you talk about them. Oh, those two young people will make out all right, but I'd have a lot more respect for them both if he didn't talk so much. Now she knows enough to keep her mouth shut, but then she was born around here and he came from Massachusetts."

"Is the right with him or with her?" I asked. "Or isn't there any such thing?"

"The wrong is as much with him as with her. That's the way it always is. Did you ever see anyone yet that was all good or all bad?"

"No—" I tried to think. "I don't suppose I have."

"Well, I have," she flashed at me, "and that's your Bill. Why such a man as he had to—" and then she stopped suddenly as if she had caught herself saying something she shouldn't say.

I was used to that. "Lose his sight?"

"Yes." Her jaws closed on the word like a steel trap. "It riles me when I think of such a fine man being so afflicted."

I tried to say to her what I had said so often to myself, that there really is no explanation for some of the things met in life. Perhaps they are the highroad to the high goal. Who can ever say? I thought of Kester, accepting one of the strangest of gifts and using it to advantage. "There are plenty of things one just can't explain," I said. "All I know is that Bill is a growing kind of person and that nothing can keep him from growing. He doesn't bother himself with what might have been. He lives in what is."

She looked at me curiously. "When I was a little girl there was a great shade tree near our house," she began, speaking slowly as she drew the words from memory. "A maple. One night it was struck by lightning and one side of it was stripped clean of branches and limbs. Much of the bark was torn to ribbons. Everyone told my father that he'd have to cut the tree down, but he said it had not received a mortal injury and he wanted to see what it would do of itself.

"He waited a year. The tree didn't die, instead it was almost as if the bolt had charged it with new life for it put on green and vigorous leaves when spring came round again. But not on the side where the lightning had struck. It never would grow there again, but where it could grow —it did!"

She fell silent for a long moment. "Odd," she began again, "but as I think back to that tree it seems as if it was the most important thing in my childhood. My swing had been on the side ripped bare, so I never swung again from that tree; but what shade there was on the other side! It was thin in the spring, deep green and cool in the summer, and when the September frosts came a half circle of white could be seen on the grass under the tree. Not the full circle, as with other trees. But a perfect half. Somehow it was much more beautiful that way." She looked at me and her eyes narrowed. "I've always loved maple shade, but I'd forgotten why until something you said about your Bill being a growing kind of person reminded me of that tree."

Sometimes our city friends asked us if country living was not dull.

"No one coming to your door from one day to another, nothing to break the monotony," Netta sighed at the thought.

"But you can't guess the number of people who come to our door!" I exclaimed.

"People you really like to see?"

"Oh, yes—" while I thought of the various ones that marked a week or a season, Bill started to describe a few of the special visitors.

One was the fishman who came on Thursdays in his homemade truck with fish fresh from the Gloucester wharves. "But almost as important as the fish we buy from him," Bill went on, "is his weather forecast given free the first of every month."

"Based on the newspapers, I suppose?" Stuart asked.

"Oh no," Bill laughed, "nothing so common as that. Based on his wife's conviction that the weather for the coming month follows the pattern set on the last Friday of the old month."

"Does it work?"

"About as well as any long-range forecast."

"And then there's the apple man," I said.

"Well, he comes only during the fall," Bill reminded me.

Whatever I bought from him, Macs and Delicious for eating, Baldwins for pies, he always gave me a dividend. He would set my purchase on the floor by the door, then reach into his pockets and give me whatever he had put in them. One day it was two jumbo Cortlands that he handed to me. "You put these in your husband's hands and just see what he says, then tell me next time I come."

I found myself hoping that the apple trees we had set out would not bear too heavily for I did not want to be deprived of the apple man's visits, and of the surprises he gave me to put in Bill's hands, as he always said, "to see what he says."

The Rural Free Delivery carrier who left our mail in the box at the side of the road was, of course, our most constant caller. His route was a long one, more than forty miles, and he did not often have time for a visit. Into the box with the mail, down with the little red flag if there had been letters for him to pick up, and off he went, the sound of his tires sucking up the road. When it was necessary for him to see us—a registered letter to be signed for, postage due, or something too large for the box like a bundle of books from the State Library, he sounded his horn as he approached. Occasionally there was nothing special to deliver but a piece of news to relay. We were relieved to know of an immediate event, a birth or a death, as the local paper came out only once a week. When he had a few extra minutes for chatting, he often told us of the wildlife that he saw on some of the back roads he traveled, and he could always be counted on to inform us of driving conditions on bad winter days.

One Saturday morning I went to the box in answer to his horn. He gave me a small handful of mail, then looked at me reproachfully, "I'm sorry to hear that you folks are moving away."

"What?"

"Selling out, leaving us. Going back to the city."

"Bill," I called, relieved to know that he was not far off. As he came toward the gate, I told him the staggering news.

"Whoever said such a thing?" Bill asked.

"Heard it in town."

"Well, it's not true. We belong here. We wouldn't sell this place for anything."

"Is that so!" The reproachful look gave way to a broad smile. "You have taken a load off my mind." He stepped on the gas and soon had roared down the road.

"Now, who do you suppose started that?" I asked indignantly.

"I don't suppose it really matters how the rumor got started," Bill said comfortingly, "because if there's one thing the RFD can do it's quench a rumor quicker than sand can fire."

Then there were the children who came to our door or on visits through the year or through the years, from the several real nieces and nephews to the ever-increasing number of those adopted by affection.

The trick-or-treaters on Hallowe'en made the briefest stay. Dressed up in masks and costumes planned weeks in advance with the express desire of horrifying, they always wanted to be sure that we knew just who was doing the horrifying.

"No, I'm not a witch. I'm Flossie."

"Don't you know me even though I am a skeleton? I'm Johnny."

"I really scared you this time, didn't I?"

They went squealing off into the darkness, trailing thank-yous behind them for the apples and cookies we had given them.

There were youngsters who fished the brook in the spring when the season opened and the water was high. They often shared with us some of their catch of rainbow trout and delighted in describing to Bill the beauty of the fish. There were boys who once had read to Bill, or come in to talk with him about dogs or baseball; now grown tall and home on vacation from college, they came in to talk with him about their new interests and plans for the future.

With them there was totality of acceptance. They did not fumble for words, they gave no curious stares as they wondered what it was like to be blind. They were near enough to imagination's realm to know. They looked at Bill with frank and open gaze, placing a warm hand in his for greeting or in guidance. Pleasure was on their faces, in the tone of their voices, that here was a person who knew how to listen, wanted to listen, and who had plenty of time. Rarely did I hear a young person say "I wish you could see it." The description given would be so vivid that he did see it.

Seven-year-old Barney, sitting on the porch with Bill one summer afternoon during a light shower, suddenly exclaimed, "I'm going to take my clothes off and run in the rain! Then I can tell you, Uncle Bill, what it feels like."

"All right, Barney. I'll watch you."

Barney pulled off T-shirt and shorts, then he ran out on to the lawn. He stood on his head, rolled over the grass, turned a few somersaults, then lay flat, soaking up the rain. When he came back to the porch, he dried himself with a towel that I had fetched for him. When he pulled his clothes on over his glowing body, he was completely satisfied with his experiment.

"It feels as if a hundred mice with little cold wet feet were running all over you, tickling you, sometimes stroking you. Uncle Bill, did you ever keep mice?"

"No, Barney, guinea pigs were my specialty."

"Is it true that guinea pigs' eyes will fall out if you hold them up by their tails?"

Bill laughed heartily and the conversation went on.

Larry, whose only knowledge of the country was gained when his parents came to see us, was intrigued by our seven shiny black hens almost identical in appearance. Finding one on the nest, he slipped his hand under her and discovered an egg which he brought gleefully to the house. A little later he said, "I'm going over to see if she's laid another egg."

Before supper he had brought in six eggs.

When he left with his parents that evening to return to the city, he held tenderly on his knees a small basket containing the six eggs. His last words were cautionary.

"Uncle Bill, I hope you won't ever eat that hen. She's a pretty good hen to lay six eggs in one day, and I practically saw her do it every time."

Apparently we had not convinced Larry that the hens took turns on the nest.

Aunt Ada spent her eightieth birthday with us in a state of indignation that life could have brought her to such a pass. She resented her years, as she had been resenting them ever since she had turned fifty. As far as I could see, she would like to have been cast at some period in life when her health was good and her friends around her and always there. Now she had come to a time when her hearing was unreliable, her sight deceptive, and her body that had been as sturdy as a horse for the greater portion of her years was beginning to make a few protests.

It was no good for anyone to point out that she was marvelously preserved for eighty. She didn't want to be eighty. She could no longer do the work she had done up to her retirement ten years ago, and she was convinced that she was finished. So many of her friends and contemporaries had taken their departure that the niches of time that had once been filled with companionship were now filled with loneliness.

I was at a loss to know how many candles to put on her cake. Eighty would only have rubbed in the bitter fact. Eight might have caused her quick mind to do some arithmetic and realize that each one stood for a decade. One might have looked as if we thought she had only another year before her.

Bill suggested three. "She can do what she likes with three as a number, and if she wants to see it as a talisman she can always remember that good things often come in threes."

"Perhaps she'll see it as a chance for each one of us to make a wish for her."

"That's a pious hope. If she does nothing at all, it won't surprise me."

Bill had for years assumed a kind of moral responsibility for Aunt Ada which relieved me greatly.

We lived through the long weekend she spent with us and heard the existing structure of the world demolished as completely as if she had her own pocket-size A-bomb. There was no use countering her, or challenging her, exposing her fallacies or trying to enlighten her. She had one rejoinder to end all rejoinders and she uttered it with ice-fringed superiority.

"My child, *you* are not eighty. You do not know what it is to be eighty. Pray God you never will."

There were times when I felt eighty-plus, but nothing was gained by saying that.

Picking up a newspaper, she would throw it down in disgust because she had not brought her glasses with her. "These days there's no news fit to read anyway," she would say. "It's entirely different for you, Bill; of course you can't see at all, but then you lost your sight quickly and you were young enough to make a reasonable adjustment. It's this slow dwindling that infuriates me."

We turned up the hi-fi until we lived in terror of cracking our ceilings, but her conviction was that there was no longer any music worth listening to.

"Have you ever thought of getting a hearing aid, Aunt Ada?" Bill asked mildly.

"Well, I may have to come to one, but I certainly don't need one yet," she retorted.

When she left I was beseiged by a sense of complete and utter failure. I had hoped that just being a part of our own peaceable home, seeing and talking with Bill, might make some change in Aunt Ada. But it had not for all the years she had been coming to visit us.

"There are people you just can't do anything for," Bill said philosophically.

"When you're young and active, I suppose you don't think of being old any more than you think of dying, but when you're eighty—"

"Well, dear Aunt Ada," Bill went on, "she's still trying to live as if she were twenty-five years younger than she is."

"Every time she leaves after a visit we talk about her in this same way."

"I know we do."

I sighed. "And we don't get anywhere."

"It doesn't look as if we could do much for Aunt Ada," Bill said, "but she does a lot for us. She makes us think ahead."

We were sitting on the porch when it happened—the sudden brilliance of light around us. It lasted for a minute perhaps, then it was gone. I uttered an exclamation, but it was not until it was over that I could explain it to Bill. The sun, reflecting on the water in the birdbath, made a shaft of light that seemed to go right through us. While it lasted, I could see nothing but the light.

"How did it happen, Bill?" I whispered, still held by the spell of light.

"It must have been the level of the water and the angle of the sun," Bill conjectured, "and something to do with our position here on the porch. It might never happen again in just that way."

"It's like one of Mary's sayings, 'Wait for the moment. All of life may reveal itself in that moment.' "

A solitary robin stood splashing in the birdbath, while two chipping sparrows waited on a nearby branch for their turn.

Either Mary or I would generally describe people to Bill. When we could, we did it beforehand so he would have a mental picture. Often they were remembered from sighted days and Bill had only to be brought up to date on the changes made by time. But there were occasions when Bill described people to us. Sometimes he was way off; at other times he was uncannily accurate.

A man and his wife, newly settled in our countryside, came to dinner one night. Neither Mary nor I had had a chance to brief Bill before they arrived, so after they had gone we asked him how he had visualized them.

"This was the way I felt about them," Bill began. "He was a squarish sort of man with a head somewhat large in proportion to his body. He wore a gray suit, and I wouldn't be at all surprised if you told me his tie was gray, too—"

"It was," Mary said, "with red rectangles scattered down it."

"She was smaller than you," Bill looked at me, "but much plumper than you, Mary, and I thought she was all of a color. Brown hair, and a sort of cocoa-brown dress. Didn't she have a way of tilting her head slightly forward when she talked?"

We nodded, then I remembered to add the word "Yes."

"Her eyes were blue, Bill," Mary said, "a slightly faded blue, like denim worn through many summers."

"Thanks, Mary. I'm really glad to see her eyes, to see some color other than the brown."

The people who came to the house inevitably brought portions of the world with them. Some were better than others at making Bill a participant in their adventures. From the first, Dan had always been one to make things possible. If he could not do it directly, as he had with the maple sugaring, he did it by way of a story that put Bill beside him in the center of the action.

One night Dan told us of a caller he had had.

"He was a little fellow I befriended last spring. Came back to tell me all was well. Left the print of his hooves in the vegetable garden. Looked like all deer tracks to me, but not so to my dog. Mike put his nose into those tracks and read them as if he was reading a letter."

"Tell me about him."

"That's what I figured to do, Bill." Dan eased himself into a chair and stretched his legs out before him. "One day last May I was driving along a back road with another man. It wasn't dark enough for lights, but the woods on either side of the road were getting shadowy. A deer jumped the stone wall on the left of us and ran across the road, her white tail high. She took ten feet at a bound and was over the right wall before we could say anything. I put the brakes on, but not soon enough to keep from hitting her fawn.

"There it lay on the road, a little orange-brown thing, covered with white spots, squealing for all it was worth, maybe not so much in pain as to its mother not to leave it. But she had disappeared. When we picked the little fellow up, I saw that one of its hind legs hung limp, so we drove to the vet as quick as we could. The fawn weighed only seven or eight pounds and he struggled for a moment in my arms, then gave up and rested his head on my shoulder as quiet as a kitten. I could feel him relax. The fear and the trembling seemed to ripple right out of him.

"You know what clever hands Doc has. He ran them over the spotted body, then the limp leg, and fingered the joint. 'I've set it,' he said. 'Now just hold him still while I get a splint on it. Those bones are so tender they'll knit in two-three days.' Talking all the while he worked, his voice must have soothed the fawn. 'You'll have to care for him as you would a lamb or a calf, but don't make a pet of him. The woods are his natural home. He'll develop what he needs and find his place with his own kind someday.'

"I asked Doc when we should let the fawn run free. 'When you see the knobs of his antlers begin to appear, you'll know he can take care of himself,' Doc said.

"I took the fawn home with me. There's no safer place than mine for a wild thing for half my acres border Sanctuary Land. In the shed by the house I filled a box with brush and dried leaves, then I set the fawn in it. He froze as obediently as if his mother had given him a command. He looked like a piece of log spotted with sunlight and he moved only when I brought him a nursing bottle of warm cow's milk. He sucked it all right, and his pleasure seemed to run right down his little body and even make his white tuft of tail quiver. Then he would respond to my hand as if it were the doe's hoof and curl up into quietness again. Even old Mike never discovered him, for a fawn is odorless in infancy.

"Four days later Doc came and took the splint off. The fawn stood on wobbly legs, but all four hooves dug sharply into the earth. He stepped daintily away from Doc, then made a leap back toward my hand that held a bottle of warm milk.

"Every day he grew stronger. He and old Mike became the best of friends and Mike shepherded him as he once had a lamb that I'd reared on a bottle. One day I left the fawn in the barnyard with a cow that had just freshened. When I came back from town, there was the cow feeding the fawn as if it were her calf. As the fawn grew more agile and his coat began to change to a red-tan color, he went often with the cows to pasture. Soon he became brave enough to venture into the woods that bordered the pasture. All day long he would be off on his own, but at night he returned to join the herd. Often of an evening I'd go up to the pasture to watch for the fawn. Sitting in the shadow of a granite boulder, downwind of the woods, I'd wait to see what I could see."

"I'll bet you were rewarded," Bill said.

"Time and time again! As dusk deepened, the fawn appeared. He was generally alone, but one evening he came from the woods accompanied by another half-grown fawn. They played like two lambs—leaping, chasing, racing, raring up on their hind legs and boxing together. Then standing square on their four legs, they'd suddenly rush each other with lowered heads, readying themselves for the day when their knobs would be antlers and they could battle in earnest.

"All of a sudden I saw the second fawn stand still, lifting his head as if his ears had caught a call or his nostrils a whiff of danger. Tossing his head, he turned and leaped over the stone wall with a whistling snort and disappeared into the woods. The other watched, then shook his head and trotted across the pasture to one of his foster mothers. But the old cow knew when the fawn should be eating grass. As the days went on she allowed him less and less milk, pushing him away with her horns. Surprised, he'd stand and look at her with his legs splayed, then drop his head to the grass or lift it to nibble some birch leaves.

"He's full-grown now and I don't see much of him, but the other evening I went down to the pond and thought to sit for a while—" Dan took a deep breath.

By the expression on Bill's face I knew that he was sitting beside the pond with Dan, waiting.

"Not one, not two, but five, six, seven deer stepped out of the woods and approached the pond. Their ears moved constantly, their heads turned this way and that. They're in the blue now and their coats are slatey-brown streaked with black and white hairs. I recognized my young buck. Almost all his spots had disappeared and where the knobs were on his head I could see small spikes beginning to show.

"One at a time the deer stepped down to the pond to drink. When they had had their fill they went back to the woods, but it was so dark then that I couldn't see them disappear, but I could hear them calling to each other— Hoo-hroo. The sound was almost like that of doves, only much stronger.

"That was more than a week ago, and last night the young buck made a call on me. I might have guessed from the prints in my garden, but Mike knew. Those scent glands in a deer's hooves are unmistakable to a dog. Mike smelled his way along the hoof prints, wagging his tail and looking at me now and again as if to say, 'Look, who's been to see us!' "

Dan drew his legs up as he rose from his chair. "Well, folks," he said, "I've got to be going, but it makes me feel kind of good to know that I've got a friend back there in the woods."

Philippa and Andy came to spend a Sunday with us. It was a quiet rainy day near summer's end. After dinner I said, "Let's go to the Acre." Everyone was agreeable, for that was one place where it never mattered what the weather did.

Bill seemed gayer than ever as we went through the woods, over the trail of flattened leaves and pine needles. Dusk came early on that mist-softened day. The trees were dripping. The pond was like a flat pewter plate and the rain was so fine that it scarcely scratched the surface. Against the green of the hemlocks stood the pale gold of maples and birches that had just begun to turn. The only sound was the dripping from the moisture-laden trees.

In the cabin we lit the kerosene lamp and the fire. Soon the birch logs on the hearth were sending their thick oily smoke up the chimney and their warmth into the room. Scrambled eggs, toast, and a big brown pot of tea were made. We got to talking about what each one of us most wanted from life. It was a long subject. We talked on and on as hope merged with desire and the longing for achievement had often to be tempered with compromise.

"And you, Bill," Philippa asked, "what is it you most want—your sight?"

Bill was silent for a moment. "In theory, I suppose, yes," he said, "but I never think of it that way. When I knew that I would not see again, I put all thought of sight —even as a wish—out of my mind."

It was ten o'clock. The fire had gone from flames to

coals, and now was only a bed of warm ashes. The night had cleared, though beyond the cabin the darkness seemed as solid as a wall. Linda, roused from sleep by the fire, was ready to lead the way out of the woods. With her nose to the ground and her lead in someone's hand, she could be trusted to get safely to the road where we had left the car.

"She'll get you out all right," Bill said to Philippa. "She knows the trail."

"But what if she gets a scent and wants to follow it? What do I do then?"

"She won't. She knows what's expected of her."

"I can scarcely see her—just those white hairs in her coat, but I can feel her tugging."

"Yield to it and put yourself in her paws. You'll get out to the road before any of us."

Tawn yawned and stretched, then stood waiting for his command. He expected to have Bill take his lead, as Bill so often did. Instead, Bill placed Tawn's lead in Andy's hand.

"Just follow that white tip of tail and you'll be all right. Go, Tawn."

Tawn looked up at Bill, wondering if he had heard right. The familiar word repeated again convinced him. Stepping carefully into the darkness, Tawn moved ahead. Within a minute, two dogs and two people were lost to us in the night.

I offered my arm to Bill, then stopped after five paces. "Bill, I can't see a thing. It's pitch black. It's—" I reached for words to describe something that he knew well.

"Take my arm," he said. "My feet know the path."

We moved forward, Bill a little ahead of me. Sometimes I could see the sudden white of a birch tree within inches of us, brushing against it brought a shower of raindrops down on us. Sometimes a huge mass loomed up before us as if to block our way, but the path went around it and the mass turned out to be a familiar boulder.

"Wait a minute," Bill said, sensing that we were off the path.

I stood still while he tried the ground with his feet until it gave back the familiar feel that he was seeking, then we went on again.

The others had reached the stone wall and were complimenting the dogs. The opening made by the road gave enough light to distinguish outlines—two people, two dogs, the car.

"That little Linda, she was wonderful!" Philippa exclaimed. "She led me without a single stumble, not a single hesitation."

"Tawn was quiet and steady, but he had to concentrate with every bit of him to do as well as Linda," Andy said.

"Didn't you have a flashlight?"

The question brought me up to reality—without star, dog, or light I had come safely through the woods.

"No, I had Bill."

EIGHT *I* *The Golden Bridge of Autumn*

S E P T E M B E R days moved on to the edge of October
and color filled our world. The turning of the leaves had
been going on all during September, until at month's end
we seemed to be living in a world canopied and carpeted
with gold. Every year it was more beautiful.

"Bill, is it really more beautiful than it was last year,
or do I just forget *how* beautiful it was last year?"

"Buttercup," he said, "that is probably one of your most
profound questions which I cannot answer."

The air was charged with some new quality. We had
gone for a long woods walk, all during which I had tried to
describe the richness and the glory that was around us. In
and among the gold of the sugar maples was the brilliant
scarlet of the swamp maples, the quieter russet of the
beeches, the deep maroon of the sumachs. The distant

mountain slopes looked as if paisley shawls had been thrown over them.

Coming up the slope from the brook, I caught sight of the mulberry tree by the stone wall set off against a clear blue sky. "Bill, it's the color of champagne, and the sun through it makes the leaves positively translucent!"

We stopped for a moment to get our breaths and drink in the color before we started across the field to the house.

"But Bill, tell me, can you possibly see all this riot of color that I've been trying to describe to you?"

"Oh yes," he said quickly, "and I need to be kept seeing it. There is a tendency for color to fade out of my mental pictures. Unless you, or someone describing things to me, revives it by vivid words I find myself seeing things in tones of gray, even though the form and structure seem clear to me. Do keep up your descriptions, they mean everything."

"Of course, you can remember color. I expect that's why it comes alive within you with a description. But what must color be for people born blind?"

Bill was silent. "It's hard to say," he spoke slowly as if he were trying to picture himself in another situation, "for color is one of the most difficult qualities to imagine." Then he laughed, "However, I once heard a blind lawyer tell a friend of his that though he could not see color he could certainly feel it. His unbelieving listener scoffed at the thought, and the lawyer asked, 'Won't you agree with me that I can feel blue?' "

The following Sunday at the Acre gave Mary and me the greatest challenge of the year as we tried to describe it to Bill. It was a mellow, dreaming sort of day. The pond, still under a cloudless sky, was bordered by multihued trees interspersed with the rich tones of the evergreens. It looked as if a Roman scarf had been lightly looped around it. A week of frosty nights had made the water too cold for swimming, but the Blueberry plied her way over the water that was in many places gold from the reflected foliage.

"Listen!" Mary said suddenly.

We listened, and searched the cloudless sky. The faint far honking that Mary had first heard, and Bill and I soon caught, told us that a flight of southbound geese was going over.

For weeks past there had been signs of summer's end. The first had been when the swallows went sometime during the third week in August, leaving the barn silent and empty and the air around the house so strangely devoid of activity. Then there had been the gradual turning of the leaves and, in mid-September, the first frost that wrote finis on the garden. And now the southbound geese— the surest sign of all that the seasons were changing. But winter was still distant. We would not reach it until we had crossed the long golden bridge of autumn that spanned the time between summer and the first real cold. Sometimes we heard geese going over at night, keeping up their constant chatter as they followed their long-established flyway; sometimes we both heard and saw them, if our ears were sharply tuned. It was one of the year's magical moments.

"There they are!" Mary pointed.

So high they were that they were almost not to be seen at all, and yet once seen they could be followed by the eye to the limit of vision. Southwestward across the sky went their beautiful, purposeful flight.

"See their wavering pattern, like a piece of gauze blown by the wind—that means they're snow geese. Canadas fly in an almost perfect V. How many did you count?"

"Just over a hundred, then I lost them."

Keeping steadily to their course, they had now gone from our sight but we could still hear their distant honking. We listened, until even that had gone.

"Do you remember," Bill asked, "that ancient Chinese scroll entitled "The Hundred Geese"? Each goose was depicted in a different way—taking off, landing on the water, swimming, feeding, preening, diving, flying—and almost every conceivable position of the wings when in flight was shown, wings which move faster than the human eye can discern?"

"Ye-es," I murmured, as I dimly recalled having seen the scroll.

"And then, centuries later," Bill went on, "when high-speed photography was developed, the different positions of the geese and their wings in flight were found to be exactly as that early artist had portrayed them."

"When did you see it, Bill?" Mary asked.

"Oh, a long time ago, years ago at an exhibition in London. I've never forgotten it. I saw it all again when the geese went over."

The day had more in store for us as clouds began gathering in the west. From the first tinge of color until the last vestige drained from the sky, Mary and I did our best to describe the sunset to Bill, though we often felt beggars for words.

Currents of vivid red and rose swept over the massed clouds and spread to the zenith. The water reflected the color in muted tones, and the trees along the shore were dyed by it to shades of plum and violet. Some of the clouds took on an apple-green tint, some became bright blue; a wash of gold spread slowly across them, deepened to copper, and gradually disappeared as twilight took over the world; then night came. There were stars in the sky and stars with ragged edges in the water.

"It must be time to go home."

We went reluctantly, but the magic went with us.

Even the brilliant sunset was a token of the season. It might be weeks before the ground froze hard, and weeks again before snow came to blanket the land, but taking Nature's hints we filled available time with a sequence of small jobs that had to be accomplished before one season gave way to another.

The garden was put to bed, which was only another way of saying that the vegetable plot was covered with a rich blanket of cow manure which Dan brought and spread for us, and the flower border had not only the manure but a neat layering of pine boughs over it. Frank and Bill were busy taking off the screens, washing windows and hanging storm sash. Then they got the winter walks from the barn and laid them from house to barn, house to road, and across the barnyard. With the walks down we were ready for any snow that might fall as they made the shoveling that much easier. Mary and I planted bulbs, adding every year a few more daffodils and narcissi to greet the spring. Cordwood, cut the previous year and seasoning ever since, was got under cover in barn and woodshed to have dry and handy for winter fires.

They were all slow, peaceful jobs. There was no rush or urgency about any one of them. They were such a contrast to the spring tasks when everything was growing, life was surging, and it was hard to keep pace with all that had to be done. The days were warm, often so warm that it was possible to doubt the approach of winter, but the mornings were generally cool and there were often frosts at night.

It was the last Saturday in October and Bill and I were working up a future wood supply as we sawed some cordwood into fireplace lengths. Linda, given more and more to slumberous meditation as her years advanced, lay curled in a little heap of leaves, blanketed with sunshine. Tawn, always alert to any need that Bill might conceivably have, sat watchfully near where we were working. Stopping for a moment, I looked around us and felt suddenly aware that color had gone from the world. Why suddenly, I could not really say, for color had been going ever since the first leaves started to drift down the wind in August.

"Now the hills look like the backs of deer, great resting deer," I said to Bill. "The gray of the tree trunks and the brown of the oak leaves give them that appearance. There's such a skeletal beauty this time of year. The bare trees look so strong. You know, Bill, I think that this is the most beautiful time of all this beautiful season, when the structure on which the glory has been hung appears for what it is—something deeply rooted with a skyward reach."

"What about the pines?" Bill had thrown his head back and was breathing deeply.

The air carried their fragrance. Standing dark and stalwart in the woods and across the hills, they gave a vital look to the whole countryside.

"The pines are magnificent," I said. "Now they seem to be coming into their own, and what stability they have!"

We lifted another log onto the sawhorse, placed the crosscut saw in position, and continued one of the smoothest and most rewarding of tasks. Draw, release. Draw, release. The saw bit its way into the wood, guided by the hands. Draw, release. The saw sat the wood as lightly as a rider a horse, and as surely. There was a lovely, lovely rhythm as the work went on. Draw, release. Draw, release. Draw—the saw had got through and the two halves of the log fell to the ground. I steadied the saw while Bill reached for the logs and tossed them onto the pile behind him.

Bill had taught me how to split wood. Putting the chunk down, I would find the run of the grain, set the wedge in it and hit the wedge with the mallet. Sometimes one blow would do it, generally it took more. There was a clean crisp sound when the wood gave and two split pieces ready for stacking lay on the ground.

"Isn't your mallet head getting loose?"

"Oh, I don't know. Is it?"

"It sounds loose to me."

I looked at it and handed it to Bill. "You're right."

"Could be dangerous." He moved his foot through the tall grass to find a flat stone on the ground. Dropping the butt of the handle against it, he drove the head home. "There," he said as he handed the mallet back to me. In the tone of his voice echoed generations of men, all careful users of tools. Ruefully I told myself that was something some women still had to learn.

Indian summer came, or so any few days of mild weather in November seemed to be called. Soft, warm, reminiscent days. Birds appeared, some of them migrants, others lengthy visitants. Bluebirds who had nested in one of the houses in June came back, still traveling as a family, parent birds and three young, to look the house over and make plans for another year. Robins spent long blissful moments splashing in the birthbath. Goldfinches swayed on the seed heads of aster and goldenrod. Pheasants churred. From the dell came the call of the white-throat; thin and rusty, it sounded like a farewell before he took wing and headed south.

The warm spell lasted so long that people began to call it "unseasonable."

Dan had a ready retort. "Whenever a good day comes, be glad for it. We always get days out of season. I've known a breath of autumn in March, and an April day in September. January thaw. August cool spell. You have to take them all, but at least you can enjoy a good day when it comes. Whenever it comes. Same as you can enjoy your life, whatever it is."

"That's what I feel," Mary said, "if you're going to live life, take it all—youth, age, joy, sorrow. Don't shy away from any of it."

The good weather held long enough to grace the wedding of two friends. We had not known the house could expand to hold so many people when, after the ceremony at the church, they all returned to Shieling. There were fires on the hearths, candles on the dining-room table, flowers, lights, and warmth as the November dusk closed in. Mary and I had made dozens of sandwiches, and plates of little cakes. Everyone gathered in the dining room and a large glass goblet, beautifully chased, with a history of more than a hundred years in the groom's family, was filled with champagne to be passed from guest to guest. Before the first sip was taken by the bride, Bill gave the toast.

He stood quietly for a moment, goblet in hand, then lifted it toward the bride and groom, saying, "May you, who are sure and strong, stand always as beacons to those who are less so. May the love on which your lives are founded grow within you so that you become more radiant as the years go on." Then he handed the goblet to the bride who sipped and passed it to her husband, and so around the group until it came back to Bill.

Long after the newlyweds had left in a shower of good wishes, long after the guests had gone and we had tidied up the house, Bill's toast echoed within me. So shining-eyed yet serious those two had been as they repeated the timeless words about sickness and health, better or worse, richer or poorer, and gave the assurance that each would cherish, comfort, and honor the other. But did they really know what they had said? Bill and I had said those same words to each other. Had we known then what they meant? In theory, perhaps; in wonderment; in the whole-souled way youth gives a promise when an immediate goal has been achieved. But did we guess, does anyone, what the promise may require? The way ahead looks as if it must be under rainbow arches because, wherever it leads, it will be followed together. Together: that was the word that held the challenge; not sickness . . . not poorer . . . not worse.

It looks so easy, this journey with another through life, for everything has been doubled—the dreams as well as the zest—and the direction seems sure and straight. But what if something happens to change the direction? What if "worse" looms larger than "better," "sickness" becomes more than "health," "poorer" takes over "richer"? From now on two are joined in a relationship with needs that deepen and grow. With it there is the promise made on a golden occasion and bound by a golden circle.

Deep in our woods was an ancient pine that I had come upon once on a walk with the dogs. I called it my bo-tree. It was a place where I liked to go alone, and think. I had reached it by pushing my way through underbrush, a tangle of blackberry bushes and the branches of storm-felled trees. The pine was immense. The wide spread of its branches had kept clear a space around it that was inches deep in pine needles. For more than two hundred years, or the length of time our particular countryside had been settled, the tree had stood there. When the forests were first cleared it had been spared, probably because of a slight twist in its trunk. No good for lumber, it had been left standing as a pasture pine. For more than a century it must have looked down on open fields, farmlands, and pastures set off by stone walls. It kept on growing.

As farming left New England and many of the fields gradually went back to forest, it had again escaped cutting because of the twist in its trunk that made it more than ever useless as lumber. Every three years it bore an enormous crop of seeds. The area all around it must have been planted by its wideflung casting, for it was coming up into sturdy pines, all second or third growth. The old pine kept on growing; not in height, for it had attained its height a century ago, but in girth and deep-rootedness. Every fall, at the snowing of the pines, it shed brown needles for new green that had been forming through the summer. It had escaped lightning, it had resisted winter damage, it had withstood hurricanes that had leveled many nearby giants.

Years and years ago, something had happened to change the direction of its growth—a small disaster perhaps, a minor tragedy; but the power to grow that resided in the tree itself had not been impaired. Had the pine grown tall and straight, as it should have done, it would have long since served the purpose of a forest tree. It grew, but in another way, and for years it had served other purposes. The forest creatures must have known it well, perhaps often finding shelter in the needle-strewn clearing under the wide branches.

When I discovered it, I doubted if any human eye had seen it for a long time. It was so deep in the woods, so difficult of approach, so guarded. I went to it at every season of the year, and in many moods. Leaning against its great corrugated bark, I never failed to find sanctuary. Beyond me, rimming me, the wind in the forest was like the sea. I stood at the center of calm.

Mary nudged me. "You've been standing there with your hands in that soapy water for goodness knows how long. Will you please get on with the washing so I can dry

and get things put away? The cups and saucers are done."

"Oh—" I turned my attention to the pile of plates.

"Whatever were you thinking about?"

"Sorry, I was a long way away. At my bo-tree."

"The old pine in the woods?"

"Yes."

"You've always said you would show it to me someday."

"I shall. How about tomorrow if it doesn't snow?"

Everything now was being done predicated on the words

"Before snow-fly." Friends came to see us and we went visiting. There would soon be snow—in flurries by Thanksgiving, in layers by Christmas, and friends wanted to be sure of one last visit before that happened. It wasn't that winter immobilized country folk—not now, with snow tires and plowed and salted roads. It was just a time-honored custom that certain things were to be done once more "before snow-fly." With us, right then, it was a weekend in Boston.

When I looked at the mountains the Saturday morning we had planned to start, I wondered if we might not be cutting our margin of time a bit close. There were clouds near the summits, and the sky looked ominous; but we left soon after breakfast.

"Have fun," Mary said as she stood in the doorway, a dog on either side of her, and waved us off.

"The mountains are like steel walls against the sky," I said to Bill as we drove off, "and the clouds have that sagging look."

"Sounds a bit as if snow were on the way."

"Perhaps it will snow and get it over with by the time we are on our way back Sunday night," I replied cheerfully.

When we reached Boston, we left the car in a garage and made sure of our hotel room for the night; then we set out to do some necessary shopping. When that was accomplished, we went to an exhibition on Newbury Street. Philippa had two of her water colors in it and I was eager to see them.

"I think I'll wait outside," Bill said when we reached the gallery, "you can tell me about Phil's work later."

"Oh, Bill, are you sure you don't want to come with me?"

"Positive. I always have lots of things to think about."

I felt reluctant to leave him, but I knew that he would enjoy the air far more than the crowded rooms, and I knew too that he would probably have far more to tell me when I rejoined him than I would have to tell him.

Once inside, I was really glad that Bill had not come. The rooms were filled with people and it was not easy even for me alone to thread my way to the particular pictures that I wanted to see.

"Bill, did I seem terribly long?"

He smiled and shook his head reassuringly. "I hope you didn't hurry?"

"I couldn't! The rooms were jammed." I nudged my arm against him so we could start walking along.

"Wait a minute, please. That door you just came through has the loveliest squeak. It's like an oboe tuning up. I've been having a wonderful time with it."

We stood still and waited. A minute passed and I began to get impatient, but not Bill.

"Really, it's worth it," Bill promised, "and we've got so much time. There, I hear someone coming. Now, listen!"

I did. Sure enough, one note after another the squeaking hinge went up the scale, faltered for a moment as the door was held open, then shuddered hastily down the scale as the door swung shut.

"Isn't that something?" Bill asked gleefully.

"Where's your famous little can of oil?"

He shook his head. "I wouldn't do a thing to change that squeak."

As we were walking along, Bill said suddenly, "Tell me, do I look like an Oliver?"

"Well, not to me, but what do you mean?"

"While I was waiting for you, I was aware that some

footsteps I'd heard coming along the sidewalk slowed down and stopped in front of me. A sweet voice said, 'Why Oliver, what are you doing in Boston?' 'But Gertrude,' I replied, 'you're a long way from home yourself.' "

"Bill, you didn't! What did *she* do?"

"There was a bit of a gasp and the footsteps went off in double-quick time."

It was fun to change before going out to dinner. Bill looked handsome in his dark gray suit and a small-figured foulard tie. I had a new dress for the occasion.

"How do you like it, Bill? It's blue-green, deep and rich like a stained-glass window, and the little buttons have curious ancient designs on them. See?"

The sensitive fingers that could draw meaning from a collection of braille dots explored the dress. Then Bill discovered on my wrist the bracelet that he had given me two years ago as an anniversary present. Light as a butterfly, his fingers felt my hair to see how I had done it. He caught the fragrance of some perfume he had given me.

"I like it. The dress. Everything. You."

We walked to a little French restaurant that we had long known well and where we could linger over the delicious meal, then we went on to the theater. Allowing plenty of time for everything, we got to our seats a good twenty minutes before the curtain was due to go up. I read the program to Bill. The play was one we had already read aloud at home so he was comfortably familiar with it. Sometimes with a play or a film when we could not familiarize ourselves with the story beforehand, we found that reading reviews or talking with friends who had seen it could help to give a mental background. There were some plays and films that we never attempted to see.

Sunday morning there was a church service, then we had dinner with Stuart and Netta. In the afternoon we went to a concert. One of the numbers, a Mozart flute concerto, promised to carry Bill into a realm of bliss.

We sat in the crowded concert hall talking together, but fell silent long before the rest of the audience did. I took my cue from Bill. He seemed to be the stillest person in the hall. Sometimes I almost envied him his ability to achieve that stillness, but it was something he had been learning for a long time. When the first strains of music came from the orchestra, I glanced at Bill. There was an expression on his face that told me he was in another world.

During the intermission, after we had taken a brief stroll and returned again to our seats, I said to Bill, "You looked as if you were going to float away during that flute concerto."

Bill smiled. "Shall I tell you a little secret?"

"Oh, please!"

"For certain compositions, I pretend that the composer is taking me away to listen to music he has heard before. This afternoon, it was Mozart who said to me that he had once heard a gorgeous flute concerto on a hilltop and now he would take me there to see if we could hear it together."

"So that's where you were!"

It was dark outside when we left the concert hall. Lights were shining on the city streets. It was damp and cold. Rain was certainly in the air.

Bill said, "I wonder if the driving is going to be a bit difficult."

"Oh, well," I felt reckless with all the joy we had had, "think of what's at the other end!" My thoughts now were all of the little house, waiting for us with its warmth and cheer, and of Mary and the dogs ready to welcome us home.

"I shouldn't be hungry for a week," Bill admitted, "after the marvelous meals we've been having, but a pot of tea and some hot buttered toast is going to taste pretty good."

"And some of my blackberry jam."

"Mary's bound to have made a cake. When does she expect us?"

"Sometime in the early evening. Whenever we get there."

It was heartening to have such a prospect, for by the time we were clear of the city rain was falling steadily. Sixty miles north, the chances were that it would not be rain.

"I smell snow," Bill said.

"Sounds as if you were becoming a countryman again. You couldn't smell snow in the city with all the fumes that fill the air."

"Nor hear it either, with all the noise."

"Glad we're going back?"

"Glad is no word for it."

"But we've had a grand time."

"Better than grand."

"When shall we do it again?"

"Next spring."

"How fast are we going, Bill?"

He did not answer immediately. "Thirty-nine, I'd say."

I looked at the speedometer. "You're right every time!"

At some point along the way the rain changed to snow. Huge, soft, wet flakes. I was glad it was not ice, though that there might be ice anywhere along the road was something to remember. I never had any anxiety for the car. Bill had had the snow tires put on some time ago, and he always saw that the car was kept in excellent running order. A slight shudder under us reminded me of the possibility of skidding. I hoped I would react quickly enough, if necessary, to steer the right way whichever it was—

against the skid? with it? It always seemed to be opposite to the instinctive thing. Steer in the direction of the skid. That was right. I must hold on to that.

"I feel so comfortable when I'm riding with you," Bill said. "You're the smoothest driver I know."

"Oh, Bill—" My hands eased their grip on the wheel. A runnel of gratitude trickled through me. I looked ahead where the snowflakes diverged in the lights of the car. The road was white. I couldn't see more than a car's length ahead, but it was a road I knew well.

"We're not going so fast now, are we, say about twenty?"

"Even less than that. Seems to be the best we can do at the moment."

"No need to make time. We've still got a lot to talk about." Bill began to develop a thought the play had stirred in him. It was something with which I could thoroughly agree so I didn't have to say much.

"M-mm," I murmured, eyes and mind really on the road.

"When people make such a point of saying they are free, comparing liberation with a former state, I think they are still tied. When a person is really free, he shouldn't even be aware of former captivity. Just a joyous involvement in life."

"Oh, quite," I agreed.

"Do you suppose the butterfly remembers the chrysalis? or the snake his sloughed-off skin? I don't."

We came over the brow of a hill. There was a long incline and at the bottom a narrow bridge. I pumped the brake slightly and shifted to low. The car was like a well-trained horse and responded to my signals. I didn't feel anxious, now, but capable. Bill's presence beside me, his confidence in my driving, had taken away my earlier feelings. We would get through the storm all right, not in our usual two hours, but safely, however long it took.

And then, before us, its lights shining across the snow, was the little house! No matter how often we came back to it, I never got over the thrill of seeing it there, waiting for us.

We drew up to the barn. Bill got out to open the door.

"Why, it has been snowing!" He felt the car, sheathed with ice and covered with snow. "How long has it been so thick?"

"Not too long."

"Why didn't you say something?"

"I didn't want to interrupt your philosophizing."

"The driving must have been rough."

"Not too bad."

Mary was at the door, standing there to welcome us just as she had to wave us off. As she opened it, the light streamed across the snow, covering the distance between house and barn. The dogs raced out, Tawn dancing delighted circles through the snow, Linda keeping to the path and yodeling her own particular kind of greeting.

Soon we were sitting by the fire waiting for the kettle to boil so Mary could make the tea. All around us was the good feel of home. There was a sweet geranium on the table which gave fragrance to the room, and a bowl of shiny red apples. Flames were curling around a maple log that would last far into the night. Outside the whisper of snow as it hit against the windowpanes could be heard.

"First snow of the year and we're here to receive it," Bill said. "I'm glad we got back in time."

"I'm glad you got back," was Mary's reply.

It was odd to think how completely the metropolitan life we once had lived had slipped from us. Delighted as we were to resume it for an occasional gay space of time, we were happier far to return to our rolling hills and friendly acres and the little house that had sheltered so much living in its near-two-hundred years. There was a peace about country living that had met Bill's need, and there was a pace that satisfied us both. We had learned not to ask for or expect things to happen quickly. Seeds had their way of growing; trees their own lives to fulfill. To have a part in enabling them to attain their best gave us the feeling that we were standing with our feet deep in the good life. Time, measured now largely by seasons, had a way of equalizing events. A severe winter often served to eliminate many grubs and pests. A dry summer forced root systems to go deeper. Heavy snows enriched the land. High winds tore dead wood out of trees, even though they sometimes ripped out young growth, too. Everything served a purpose. To accept what happened and use it to advantage, or make the best of it, was the countryman's point of view. And it had become ours.

For several years Bill's work had put strenuous demands on him and his time, but now there was someone on the agency staff to whom much of the responsibility could be delegated. It became possible for Bill to devote a little more of his time to personal projects.

"Why don't we take a long trip?" I asked him one evening. "We've always talked about going to San Francisco. Wouldn't it be exciting to *go?*"

Bill was silent, when he spoke he was very serious. "Yes, it would be, but there is so much frustration involved with blindness that I just don't let myself get excited about anything unless there is a pretty good chance to accomplish it."

I regretted my hasty words. "That must be true, Bill. Sometimes I wonder if I have ever wholly understood the depths of the frustration."

"Often," Bill went on, "when I'm alone, it seems as if dozens of desires and impulses spring into thought, but I can't follow up on them. Gradually I am learning to dismiss the things I can't do and to get my satisfaction from the things I can do. Some things can wait, then I ask you or Frank or Mary to help me."

I nodded and then remembered to add the words that would let Bill know I understood.

"You can see why I don't get excited about San Francisco. Right now it seems too unlikely."

But before many months had passed, Bill did begin to get excited. From a standpoint of his work, and mine too, we were able to take a real vacation.

We went by train to San Francisco where we spent a week. The sunny days, crisp air, charm of the city and kindness of friends gave us great joy. Everyone seemed to want to do things for Bill, from bus drivers, to waiters, to helpful people encountered on the street. It seemed to me that blindness had a way of opening doors and that people did things which, in the ordinary way, custom or shyness might have barred them from doing.

The day we purchased tickets for the bus tour to Muir Woods, the man at the counter looked at us closely. He had seen us twice before, but this time he clearly intended to have his curiosity satisfied.

"Excuse me, sir," he said, placing his hand on Bill's for a moment, "but do you mind my asking what you get out of this?"

Bill laughed. "Do you mind if I come in after the trip? I'll have more to tell you then."

"Not at all, not at all. I'll be here until six o'clock and the bus should get you back by five."

Over the Golden Gate Bridge and through an enchanting countryside we drove, and all the time I kept thinking how much more I was seeing as I saw for Bill and tried to describe things to him in vivid words. We walked through the redwoods with a guide and the rest of the people from the bus. Every few minutes we stopped while portions of an informative lecture were given and we were made familiar with the history of the trees in general and certain particular trees. My eyes traveled up their great trunks.

"Bill," I whispered to him, "they just seem to go up and up, arrow straight, and so green. They're like people, real presences."

"I know they are. I can feel their majesty."

After a while the group dispersed and we were alone with the trees. We walked slowly along the course of a stream with silence around us, breathing deeply the clean damp air.

During more than twenty-five hundred years the redwoods had gone quietly on fulfilling their cycle, doing what they had been made capable of doing with the materials at hand: the fog that came rolling in from the Pacific gave moisture for their leafy crowns, the soil provided the right nutrients for their growth. They had resisted fire. They were impervious to blight. They did one thing well: they grew. And they went on growing, not only in Muir Woods but in the hearts of all who saw them, who walked among them.

"I could really go home now," Bill said, "even if we don't see another thing. The Big Trees have filled me with content."

Before returning to the bus, we stopped at the little gift shop for a cup of coffee. Bill waited outside while I went in. The tables were crowded, so I asked one of the assistants if I might take a cup of coffee out to my husband, and I told her why.

Her kind face almost undid me. "Lovey, you go right back to him and I'll bring a tray out there to you. Two coffees, and how about a couple of pieces of apple pie?"

This sort of thing had happened time after time, as blindness drew out of people their kindest selves.

Back at the hotel in San Francisco, Bill apparently satisfied the man at the desk who had sold us the tickets to Muir Woods. I never knew what he said as I went up to our room ahead of Bill, but the next morning the man told us of tours to other places he felt we should not miss.

When we left San Francisco we took the train down the coast of California, making stops of a few days each at Carmel and Santa Barbara. We saw fertile watered fields where garden produce for the nation was grown the year around. We stood on rocky cliffs where the sea crashed below us and the air was sharp with the scent of eucalyptus. We walked for miles along sandy beaches and filled our pockets with tiny shells. We strolled slowly through the streets of venerable towns, listening to the sound of bells from the old missions, bells that carried the romance and memories of the Spanish padres. At night the air was fragrant with pinyon pine, a new scent to us.

When we took the night train from Los Angeles, I felt that my mind was lined with glowing pictures, enough to think about for years to come.

Standing on the South Rim of the Grand Canyon the next day, I knew why, when Mary had stood there two years before, she had sent us a telegram with the one word "Speechless."

We walked along the rim, took a sight-seeing bus, listened to a lecture, visited a museum, watched an Indian dance, then sat on one of the stone benches to drink in the tremendous spectacle that reached before us. During the heat of the day the high sun had flattened distant aspects; now, in the late afternoon, the sun created a changing pattern of shadows. Opposite canyons came alive with shifting colors. Below us, the great depth looked dark and mysterious. We sat still long enough to let the Canyon speak to us in its own way. It was nearly dark when we went back to the hotel for dinner.

The next day I went down the Bright Angel Trail on mule back. Bill said that he was glad to be alone for a while, that he needed to be. Our hotel room overlooked the rim and he assured me that, given time and solitude, he felt that he could become some part of the beauty and immensity around him.

"Hour by hour," he said to me late that afternoon when I returned, "I perceived more acutely what the Grand Canyon was, in its scope, and color, and age. I thought I knew what quietness could be, but this—why this seems to have all the quietness of the ages in it."

I told him of my day.

"I could imagine you 'way down on that narrow ledge," he said. "I could feel the fifteen-hundred-foot drop, or was it more? And I went with you back through the aeons recorded on those rock walls."

"The day didn't seem too long?"

"Long!" he exclaimed. "It wasn't nearly long enough."

We left the next morning, glad for the days on the train that would give us time to sort out our experiences and relive some of them all over again. We spent hours in the Dome Car and I described to Bill the vast expanses of the plains, often empty save for the cloud shadows that rested over them. Once we saw a herd of antelope, streaking along almost as fast as the train. Flocks of sheep grazed undisturbed by our passage, herds of Herefords took no notice of us. Sometimes a cowboy brandished his hat to the passing train; and once, when we were in the agricultural country, a lone farmer driving his tractor over what looked like a ten-mile-long field of corn, waved to the train and we waved back.

During dinner in the dining car on our last night, Bill announced that he was glad he lived in New England.

"Why, exactly, after all the lushness and beauty we've seen in California?"

"That's it, exactly. I think I'd miss a touch of the grindstone."

A little later Bill said, "It's wonderful what this trip is doing for me. I can see that what our agency needs right now is a mighty good recreation program."

"Bill," I exclaimed, "you're not home yet and you're already making plans for your work!"

He smiled at me. "It wouldn't really surprise me, Buttercup, if you said you were doing the same thing."

It was true, for all the time that I had been enjoying the trip, I had been gathering ideas and entertaining them in my mind. I was as eager to get back to my desk and start work again as Bill was to return to his office and commence implementing a whole new program for the agency.

"Home is where one starts from—" T. S. Eliot's line sang within me as the train wheels sang over the roadbed. I could hardly wait to get home.

> We must be still and still moving
> Into another intensity—

On and on went the sound of the train wheels. On and on.

NINE ⚡ *And That Other Bridge*

THE house was quiet. Mary was away for the day. Bill was working in his office with Frank. Even the dogs had taken themselves into some secret corner and were sleeping the afternoon away. It made me feel good to know that Bill was across the lawn in the little building that had once been too small for his activities and was now just right in size.

Bill was at home these days more often than he was away. With Frank still to help him, he was beginning to devote his time to community interests and personal plans which had long been deferred. As an officer of the agency, his interest in it was a continuing one; but after he returned from the West and had seen the recreational program get well under way, he asked his Board of Directors to release him from the administrative duties. There was a staff member ready and able to assume them, and Bill felt that it was time for another to take over. Free from the daily demands, Bill could now give his thought to long-range plans for the agency that he wanted to help shape and develop.

Behind him lay nearly a decade of devoted service with its rich rewards. The realization of all that had been accomplished during those years seemed to fill the Revere Bowl that the Directors had given Bill. To me, what the silver bowl said as it caught a shaft of sunshine or reflected candlelight, was that Bill in his help to others had found his own best way.

Looking across the lawn, I sighed with joy that Bill was near enough if I needed him for anything; or if he needed me.

I was feeling particularly domestic that day and thought to make some bread. While the dough was rising, I decided to take advantage of the brief hours of winter sunshine and the unusual mildness to plant a few more bulbs. I had noticed that there was a basket with some bulbs in it on a shelf in the cellar and wondered how Mary and I had ever missed it when planting a few weeks earlier. It seemed to me that to have an array of daffodils on the west side of the house would be a lovely thing, under the guest room windows and visible to anyone passing on the road. I dug a series of holes and tucked the bulbs carefully into the earth. To make doubly sure of their growing well, I spread a little fertilizer around them then covered the whole area with some new loam, raking it neatly.

By the time I got back to the house, the dough had risen enough so I could shape it in to loaves. I did some house-cleaning until the loaves were ready for the oven. Such domesticity made me feel virtuous. As the loaves were baking, I sat down to read the local paper that had come earlier in the mail.

That weekly paper was never anything to be hastily scanned. People read it in its entirety and its news made general conversation among townsfolk for several days. I didn't get to the New Arrivals, or to the Cards of Thanks, or to the Editor's Column or the Traffic Violations. I didn't even get to reading the list of Events for the Week. No, I didn't get beyond a single item of news and that was the death of Sarah Whin at her niece's in New Jersey. I read the notice three times and then I put the paper down.

Glancing out of the window, I saw that Bill had just left his office and was starting across the lawn toward the house, walking briskly a dozen paces, then slowing up to feel for the flagstones that led up to the door.

"Something smells good," he said, as he came in to the house.

"I'm making bread."

He stood in the kitchen doorway. "What's the matter?"

"Why?"

"You don't sound very cheerful."

"Oh, Bill, I've just read in the paper that Sarah Whin has gone at last!"

"I'm sorry to hear that, but it has been expected for quite a long time, hasn't it?"

"Yes, of course it has. I know she's had a full life, and she was in her nineties. But Bill, after all the things she once did for the young people in this town, her death is reported in just six lines."

"Well, what's wrong about that?"

"It—it makes her seem so insignificant."

Bill gestured toward the oven. "How's your bread?"

"Oh goodness, I'd almost forgotten it!" I opened the oven door. The loaves were brown, so I took them out and set them on a rack to cool.

"There must be plenty of people doing good things every

day who don't worry much about their work being known," Bill said. "They're satisfied with what comes of what they do."

"Yes, I know, but it seems to me that when a person does as much for a community as Sarah Whin once did for this community that there should be some kind of public appreciation."

"Maybe there will be in time." Bill put his hand out for one of the kitchen stools, then he straddled it. "You'd never turn out bread like that without yeast, would you?"

"No, I wouldn't." I had begun to run water into the dishpan, but I shut the water off so I could listen to Bill.

"Yeast does a good job, and then it loses itself in the grand result. Don't you think some people are like that?"

"I—I don't know."

"Sarah Whin must have felt all right as she saw the boys and girls she'd helped grow up turn out well. She's satisfied. Let's hope we'll be when our time comes."

I looked out of the window, thinking about what Bill had said. It began to make sense to me, quite a bit of sense. "I see what you're getting at, Bill."

"How about a piece of bread," he said, "with some butter on it, and maybe a cup of tea?"

"Bread won't be cool enough to cut for a few minutes. Have you got the time?"

"Why, of course I have!"

It was a foolish question for me to have asked. If there was one thing that Bill was rich in it was time. Time for what was important, and getting me straightened out just then was more important to him than anything else.

"You must have come over from the office for something, Bill. Don't let me put you entirely off your track."

"Yes, I did, come to think of it. I came over to look up a word in my Vest Pocket Dictionary."

"Better do it now. Give me five minutes and I'll have a cup of tea ready and some new bread cut and buttered."

Bill's Vest Pocket Dictionary consisted of seven large braille volumes and lived on the shelf in his bedroom.

After we had our cups of tea, and the bread that tasted so good we made one loaf look rather small, Bill said, "What's for dinner?"

"I was thinking of a stew?"

"Have you got everything you need?"

"Yes. Frank brought in the last of the carrots the other day, and we still have a few onions left. Carrots are in the frig. Onions are down cellar."

"If you'll give me something to put them in I'll go down to get them for you. I want to check on that curious noise the oil burner's been making lately. Haven't you noticed it?"

"No," I said sadly, "or if I did, I'm afraid it didn't mean anything to me." I handed Bill an empty bowl and he went to the cellar.

Well I knew that the house could come down on my ears if I were responsible for the functioning of its mechanical parts. It wasn't that I didn't hear the unusual sound, it was just that I didn't realize how indicative of something wrong it could be. It was the same with the car. Bill heard and knew the importance, traced the trouble back to a solution or got someone to do it for him.

"No onions anywhere," he said, returning to the kitchen.

"Isn't there a basket on the shelf, over at the left, above the egg crock?"

"There's a basket, but it's empty."

"Empty? It can't be." I thought back to when I had last seen the onions.

"What now, Buttercup?"

"Bill," I gasped, "I planted them! I thought those few remaining onions were daffodil bulbs."

"Can't you dig them up? Frank could do it if you'd show him where."

"I did such a good job covering them, no one could possibly find them," I groaned. "Well, we'll have the stew another day. I'll have to dream up something for tonight."

Bill closed the door behind him. A moment later he opened it again and, with a broad smile, said,

"As you'd shun the eager beaver who never has a minute,
So let's skip the steaming stew without an onion in it."

I watched Bill as he went down the flagstones, through the barnyard gate and toward his office. When I turned back to do the dishes, my eye again caught the item about Sarah Whin in the paper that was lying on the kitchen counter. I could look at it now quite peacefully. It didn't bother me any more what the paper hadn't said. I was glad I'd known her, glad she'd been in my world. She had been one of our first friends when we had come to the country to live; not near enough to be a neighbor but she had the neighbor's heart. There must have been plenty of others in the town, and even beyond the town, who had good cause to remember her, and who were happy because they had known her.

Something that Sarah Whin had said to me the first time I met her came back to me. It was while the work was being done on our house and before we had put down any but the most tender roots. " 'He who goes into strange lands falls into the hands of God,' " she had said, with a smile that made her face look like a wrinkled apple. I did not know quite what she meant, but the years were to teach me.

Looking back over them, I knew that I would not want

to surrender a single one. Sometimes it seemed as if it had been only a day since we had stood on the porch, gazed at the mountains, and planned what we would do with our acres and our lives. Sometimes it seemed as if it must have been forever. Our land was fulfilling its time-honored function as it produced crops and supplied pasturage. We were keeping faith with the first farmer who had cleared the land and built the house, and we hoped that he would approve of our husbanding. Our lives had fallen into patterns of usefulness. When Bill had first lost his sight, I wondered if I would ever be able to get through life. It was then that I began to realize what Sarah Whin's words meant, "He who goes into strange lands falls into the hands of God."

The years had been moving on. Often they merged without an apparent sense of time, until something happened that made us aware that time took its toll: something like Sarah Whin's death, or something that went almost unnoticed.

When Linda had been born we had counted five white whiskers on her chin. The rest of her was silky black which became shaggy, thick, and tough, as a true terrier's coat should be. Gradually a grizzle crept into her coat. A few white hairs appeared down her back, across her shoulders and on her undertrimmings. The time came when all the whiskers on her chin were white. Sturdy, stoic, brave, and intensely alive, she kept guard over the house, responded to an invitation for a walk with joyous barks and wagging tail, treated guests as if they were her special care, and otherwise went her own way. Accepting what was her duty, she always made it quite clear that it was her life she had to live and that everything else was done if it fitted in with her plans.

She was part of our life, Bill's and mine, but most of all

Mary's. Then we realized that age was laying its hand upon her gallant spirit. Sight and hearing became less sharp; joints began to stiffen; at times her breathing was labored.

"She's always been so gay, so alive—" Bill said.

"Somehow I thought this couldn't happen to her—" I said.

"As long as I've been with you, she's—" Mary did not finish her sentence, as we had not finished ours.

Now, in the early mornings when I watched from my bedroom window the sun rise above the line of mountains, I felt the value of each day.

> . . . *but every hour is saved*
> *From that eternal silence.*

Tennyson's *Ulysses* again was like a hand in mine.

Linda, with the quality that had marked her since she first made her appearance in the world, accepted the present pattern of life. She curled up for longer periods of sleep on her cushion or by the fire. She sat with a far-off look in her eyes, not seeing us but seeing something. No longer was it chipmunk or mole against which she had kept unremitting watch; it might have been, for all we knew, the distant shore that her small vessel was approaching.

Occasionally she showed spurts of interest in our activities, but for the most part her days were marked by a great and enveloping quiet. She was like a candle with just so much more wax to burn, yet as long as the wax lasted the flame would be bright.

I ached at the things that were becoming memories, that one by one had to be set on a shelf like books when read —her high caroling, her romps with Tawn, her joy in food, her bravery; the chase in the woods that she had reveled in; the days at the Acre when she had sat like a captain in the bow of the Blueberry. They were all finished now. She slept for long, long hours. She sat in the sun, ears alert but eyes dreamy. What little she ate, she did only to please us.

There was nothing the vet could do, but we took her to him occasionally. Bill wanted to be sure that she was not suffering.

"She's a marvelously preserved dog," the vet said, "but time has overtaken her. Do you realize that she's comparably through her eighties?"

"Then a year for a dog really is like seven for a human?"

"Yes, it's about that. You've had her a long time. She's had a full, good life, but—" he shook his head and his hands stroked Linda tenderly, "I don't think she'll see another spring."

A long life—what did he mean? It seemed no time at all since that night when she was born, and her rowdy puppy days might have been yesterday, so clearly could we recall them. What had happened to all the years of her stouthearted companioning? Where had they gone?

The first snow had run off and the ground was moist. Unwillingly I knew that a small grave should be dug while the ground could still be worked. It could be boarded over. Perhaps it would not be used for a long time. The heart could hope while the hands did necessary work.

When Bill and Mary had gone to town on some errands, I got a spade from the barn and called to the dogs. We crossed the field, went over the stone wall and halfway down the slope to the brook. A wide-branched pine stood there. I had often sat under it with the dogs on summer days. Tawn raced gaily ahead. Linda followed slowly. Finding a little bush that suited her, she settled down to watch what I was doing.

The ground gave readily to my spade; but soon frost

would lock it, snow would cover it, and it would not be soft again until spring. Linda, who had always had such contact with the earth, must have this last courtesy of the earth, and on her own land. Every now and then I glanced over at her, but she was not seeing me. Her eyes were on that middle distance. Tawn came and watched me questioningly; then he went to Linda and sat down beside her, curling himself in a prearranged fashion so she could rest her long nose on his golden back.

When we walked up the slope again and over the stone wall, I carried Linda. The once sturdy body that housed such a stalwart spirit had become quite light. I set her down carefully near the house, then went to the barn to put away the spade.

Not many days later, Linda fell into a deep blissful sleep as she lay in her basket by the fire. Relaxed and comfortable, even her breathing, that had been labored, came easily. As the day began to wane and about the time of the first star's shining, she stirred and looked at us, settled down again, and on a great tide of sleep left us.

Later that night we carried her box to the place prepared for it. There was a full white moon overhead. The brook was rushing through the night, filling it with sound. The air was frosty.

"Companionship," Bill said, "is probably the most precious of all relationships. Whether it be that of a person or a small gallant dog is immaterial."

Tawn rose to his new position, as if Linda had told him what would be expected of him.

We heard from a friend whom we had not seen for a long time. We knew she had not been well; we did not know that her doctor had given her little hope. She had been urged to get away from the city and be in the country. She asked us in her letter if we could possibly consider having her stay with us for a few months during the winter. We talked it over that night and agreed that this was one of the things a home should stand for.

Stella came within a week. She required no special care other than a breakfast tray, warmth, quiet, and an occasional routine visit from the doctor. Companionship was her best therapy. She spent her mornings in her room, reading and writing letters; her afternoons in the sunshine on the porch; her evenings with us. Stella had almost no relatives at all, only a distant cousin in some distant part of the country, but she soon became part of our life.

"Shieling is a family," Mary said to her.

"And a shelter in any kind of weather," I added silently.

There were some days, when Stella sat on the porch, that she did no more than watch light and shadows changing, shifting across the snow as the sun followed its course; but by her description to us that night at supper of all she had seen she might have been watching a circus parade. One evening she told us of the network of tunnels the current squirrels had under the snow.

"I saw Rufus's head come popping up here and there, out of the white crust, and soon realized that his means of rapid transport would be the envy of many a city subway system."

There were constant items of interest about Sambo that she relayed to us. His ingenuity called forth her admiration. It might have taxed our credulity had we not observed him, or his ancestors, on many another occasion.

"Any news of Rufus?" Bill would ask Stella at supper. "And what has Sambo been up to today?"

"I didn't see Rufus, but do you know what Sambo did? He had just started to enjoy that big doughnut you put on the bird tray, Bill, when Tawn barked in the house. It alerted him and he decided that he had better take to the woods. Intentionally or not, he slipped his head through the doughnut and ran away wearing it around his neck."

Bill spent a great deal of time with Stella, often having luncheon with her on the porch. When it was necessary for him to be away for the day, he tried to get back in time to spend an hour with her in the late afternoon. Often she read to him, but not for long periods as her strength had its limits. Sometimes Bill read to her from one of his braille books. Generally they talked, and each one had the rare capacity of being able to be happily silent in the other's company.

"If there's one thing Bill gets a person to do, it's to embrace the fullness of life," Mary said to me over our bowls of soup in the kitchen while Bill and Stella had their luncheon trays on the porch.

"Yes—" I was going to say more when a burst of laughter from the porch reached us.

"That's just what I mean," Mary nodded. "Right on the edge where Stella is now, they laugh together as if there were nothing else to do."

It was the medicine I had seen work before, and Bill had used it first of all with himself.

One afternoon when the sun was warm and icicles hanging from the eaves were dripping musically, I took a tea tray out to Stella on the porch to sit with her for a while.

She looked up from the book she was reading. "Thought I smelled something good."

"Molasses cookies," I said, "newly baked and still hot."

Her eyes seemed wonderfully clear, almost as blue as the sky behind her. "You're looking very well today, Stella," I said.

"And shouldn't I be! With nothing to do but enjoy the world around me and relish the kind care I'm receiving."

She took the cup of tea from me, and then a cookie.

"How is it," she said, "that I seem to be seeing and hearing so much lately? It's not just that I look at things more closely so I can tell Bill about them, it's something different."

"Mary and I feel it, too."

"Bill seems to have made me aware of the world in which I live. I feel tender to so many things—to you, because you're a human being like me, and to Rufus, over there, because he's a squirrel! And to that little bird. Look at him." She nodded toward a chickadee who had alighted on a nearby icicle. Clinging to it, the chickadee drank from another icicle the small drop of moisture that had formed at its tip and was about to fall.

"There've always been squirrels and chickadees and people in the world," Stella went on, "at least I suppose there have been for quite a long time, but I seem to be really aware of them now, as if we were all related to one another."

The chickadee left the icicle and flew to the evergreen hedge at one side of the porch. Stella put out her hand with a bit of cookie flat on the palm. Making his cheerful sound, the bird hopped to her shoulder, then on to her palm, took the cookie crumb and flew off with it.

"See what I mean!" Stella exclaimed. "This couldn't have happened unless I had learned to be still, and to care. A year ago I would scarcely have seen that little bird had he come as near to me as he did then, and it wouldn't have occurred to me to think that he might be hungry. Isn't it wonderful?"

"Yes," I said, and echoed, "wonderful."

We were silent for a long time and I was just about to gather the tea things together to go inside with the tray when Stella said suddenly, "Oh, there's so much more that I would like to do and see in the world, but I can accom-

plish quite a bit right where I am because I can reach—"
she paused. She looked at me in that way Linda used to
when she wasn't seeing me at all, "beyond the visible."
Leaning back in her chair she closed her eyes.

After a while she spoke in a faraway sort of voice, "It's
odd this bond one begins to feel with the rest of creation.
It doesn't always happen, you know. Sometimes bitterness creeps in and blurs things. Once I felt such utter dis-

appointment about my life. Now, somehow, I don't. I'd much rather go on living. I don't want to die any more than any one does, but I don't feel as helpless as I once did. Death is something I've got to go through, that's all. I have no apprehension about what's ahead. I'm even getting a little curious."

She smiled at me, but her eyes seemed to have lost their color.

"Bill told me such a lovely story yesterday about a visiting French organist whom he once knew. Did you know him?"

I shook my head.

"Apparently, in a conversation on the subject of immortality, a very sophisticated young woman in the group kept insisting that there was no future life. The organist asked, 'Do you really believe that?' 'I am positive,' she said. Wagging his finger at her and smiling, he said in his broken English, 'You will have surprise.' "

That was the last day Stella spent on the porch. For a week she did not leave her room, and then for a few days she did not leave her bed; but she never lost her light heart or her strength of spirit. Before she left us, she asked if she might write in our guest book. We brought to her the small leather-bound book that held the record of friendly visits throughout the years. In it she wrote, "For my New England interlude, gratitude beyond all telling."

And then there was the Big Maple.

It was as perfect a tree as we had ever seen. It had been planted about a century ago near the front gate and it had grown sturdily through the years. When we bought the house it was in its prime. It would have taken another century in its stride. People often stopped to look at it, to take pictures of it, especially at the time of high color. Once an artist spent a whole day painting it. The birds loved it. We profited by its great circle of shade in the summer months, by the leaves that enriched our compost heap, and its beauty. It was one of us. We loved it. We spoke of it in as familiar terms as if it were a member of the family.

When the town water line was put down our road we did not know that part of the maple's far-reaching root system had been injured. But it had. It took three years to show the extent of the injury, so tough was the great tree's hold on life. The following spring, the tree did not leaf out as it should; as the season advanced, dead wood appeared among its branches. We called on the tree man. He looked at it, studied it, and shook his head; but he said there was a chance, just a chance, that the injury to the root system might not have been mortal.

The maple was fed heavily and pruned vigorously. Everything was done to save it. On the third spring it hung out from its branches almost more seeds than leaves. Clusters of them hung in the sun, swayed in the breeze, and were scattered far and wide by the wind. We were elated.

"That must be a good sign," we said to the tree man.

"It's a sure sign," he answered. "A seed tree will do that at the end as if it wanted to make certain of survival of its species."

That summer more dead wood appeared. Branches that had leafed out bravely early in the season withered by mid-July and dried leaves littered the grass. We knew the tree would have to go.

Dan came by on the winter day when the tree men were working with power saw and axes. The great maple lay prostrate. "It must be like having a death in the family," Dan said. He shook his head, "Too bad, but you'll feel its warmth in your fireplaces for many years to come."

I saw Dan look up and across the road.

"I want to show you something," he said.

We followed him across the road and stood near the stone wall.

Dan put his hand on a slender maple sapling growing there. Its tip reached a foot or so above our heads. Its diameter might have been a little better than an inch.

"Come spring," Dan said, "when a tree can be moved, I'll set this youngster right beside the big one's stump."

We called the sapling Junior. It was, in all probability, one of the seeds cast by the Big Maple. It looked slim and willing. It had no personality at all. But we supposed that, given time and the elements that constituted growth, it might become a worthy successor to its parent.

Mary was watching the men as they sawed and split the huge pieces of wood, then loaded them in their truck for stacking in the barn. "I want to find a well-shaped piece with an interesting grain," she said. "I want to carve it into something for Shieling to have even long after the rest of the wood has gone in burning."

There were three who would not see the spring again—Linda, Stella, and the Big Maple. We were talking about them as we sat by the fire that night. Bill had commented on life and how each served in its peculiar way.

"And few things serve more than true friendship," Mary murmured.

Then I added my favorite line from William James, " 'The great use of life is to spend it for something that outlasts life.' "

TEN ✦ *The Candle of the Year*

WINTER finally came with frozen ground covered by snow, a succession of cold days and colder nights. On one particular night, rain turned to ice and softly falling snow before morning. When we looked from our windows we might have been in another world. The pine trees, their branches weighed down by ice and overlaid with snow, were like pagodas. The mountain that rose in lone splendor in the west might have been Fujiyama wearing the year's white mantle.

I tried to describe it to Bill as the newly risen sun shone on the ice-encased, snow-covered landscape; but words could do little to convey reality.

"Remember that moonlight climb we made once in Switzerland, Bill, when the Wildhorn looked like the walls of an ice fortress?"

Bill narrowed his eyes as if to focus inner sight. It was the way he had looked in the days when he had so often held a camera to his eyes.

"Yes, I can see the mountain, in fact the whole journey as if I were taking a series of photographs—the line of the chalet against the slope behind it when we closed the door and started out, the way the path looked all dappled with moonlight and shadows, the water as we crossed the little bridge over the Turbach, and the view as it gradually widened before us."

He was silent for a moment, then a smile came to his face and he opened his eyes wide. "I can see it all quite clearly now—that impregnable white wall of the Wildhorn!" He turned to me. "Oh, keep me seeing like that. Keep the pictures alive in me."

All during the morning the air resounded with gentle tinkling, like the cowbells we had heard so often on Swiss mountain slopes, as ice loosened its hold on twigs and branches and fell to the ground. Often the tinkling was near at hand, sometimes it was distant by a field or it came from the woods across the road. By noon the pines had freed themselves from snow and looked again like our familiar trees instead of eastern temples.

After luncheon we started in on some shoveling. Just as we were finishing up with the heavy wet snow in the driveway, Dan came by. The wheels of his truck slushed to a stop. His cheeks were as red as his coat. His voice was robust.

"Well, we're in for it," he said cheerfully.

"What?" I asked.

"Weather."

Bill leaned on his shovel. "Got time to come in and sit for a spell, Dan?"

"Time," Dan chuckled, "that's the one thing I've always

got." He reached down into the truck for something, then followed us in to the house.

"Had more apples than we could use," he said, as he set a jug of cider down in the kitchen, "so I pressed out a few gallons. Thought you'd like to have one."

Bill and Dan went in to the living room to sit by the fire. I poured some of the cider into glasses, put oatmeal cookies on a plate, and joined them.

"By all the signs," Dan was saying, "it looks as if it might be a hard winter—the woolly bears were out early, the chipmunks and squirrels have been working overtime to lay in their stores, the cows have got the thickest coats ever. But, if you want to know what I think I'll tell you," he paused.

We waited expectantly.

"I think we're going to have about the same kind of winter we generally get in these parts, four months of it, too, and a wedge into April for good measure. Plenty of snow. Two or three ice storms. Some below zero nights, and any number of good, clean, cold, sunny days. There'll be a few blizzards to keep us from getting soft, and there'll be some really bad days when the best thing folks can do is stay home. But, if anyone wants to take the trouble to add up the good days against the bad, he'll find there are a lot more good in any season. Just like last summer! We had a harvest all right, even though during that dry spell it looked as if we wouldn't get anything but radishes. Whatever the weather thinks up to do, I'll take a four-season climate to live in."

We agreed.

"You folks all set for winter?"

Bill enumerated the jobs that had been done.

"If you're ready beforehand you can come to grips with anything," Dan said. "It's when winter strikes before

you've had a chance to realize it's even coming—" he shook
his head and told us of a September snowstorm he remembered. "Cattle and sheep were in the fields, garden truck
was still out. Man, we had to work some the next day!"

As Dan had predicted, one storm followed another and
the snow piled up over our countryside. The town plow,
clearing the roads after successive storms, soon had built
up five-foot walls along the highways. There was no traveling now across the fields or through the woods except
on snowshoes. The snow came up to the sills of the
ground-floor windows of the house. It covered stone walls,
and draped fantastic white sheets over granite boulders.

After a night of snow, shoveling-out took priority. Bill
did the doorstep and the area leading up to it while I
started on a path to the gate and the mailbox; then we were
both ready to work on the longer path to the barn.

"Bill, you've got to toss it a lot higher," I said, as one of
his shovelfuls landed back on the cleared path.

"You show me."

I took his arm and moved it in the right direction.

"I get it, higher-and-farther."

The words became a rhythm to which we worked.
Higher-and-farther. Every now and then we leaned on our
shovels to rest.

"There's a crowd of little birds around the feeder, Bill."

"When we get the path cleared I'd better fill it up again.
Got plenty of seed on hand?"

"Yes, and I'll get more when I go in to town."

"*If* we get the driveway opened up."

That was the last shoveling we did. It was always the
heaviest. There were times when, just as we had it all
cleared, the plow would come by to widen the road and
with a great spray of snow from its orange wings fill the
lower half of the driveway again. The men in the cab

waved their mittened hands and grinned at us, and we waved back.

Winter was an adversary to be stood up to, there was no doubt about that. It threw down a challenge which everyone had to accept, not only the weatherwise and the fun-loving. It gave battle, but it gave as well a fair chance of emerging victorious. There was no denying the secret thrill felt at night when the mercury dropped below zero. Ten, twenty degrees below—that happened often during the winter; and there had been one memorable morning when we had seen our thermometer at minus forty-five. The trees in the woods across the road protested, snapping and crackling. The sounds echoed like shots in the stillness. All night long the house had been protesting as a rafter contracted, then another. The muffled booms were like prisoned thunder, but there were no telltale marks for what happened happened inwardly. On very subzero nights, no matter what mechanical heat the house had, there were only two really warm places—bed, or sitting close to a blazing fire. The release of years of summer heat stored up in logs of apple or maple alone seemed to get into the bones and counteract the cold.

"It's seasonable," was the remark heard most often, and then the companion, "It's healthy."

By country standards, the colder the winter the healthier it was, providing the ground was covered with a thick blanket of snow.

"Some folks go to Florida," Dan said, "but that's one thing I've never had the time to do."

The days had been shortening noticeably. It was Bill who put the house lights on every afternoon that he was home, knowing the time by his braille watch and estimating the extent of duskiness as winter days advanced. Sometimes he forgot and had to be reminded, sometimes he put them on too soon, but "lighting-up" was one of the many household assignments that he had taken over and I depended on him to do it. During November he put on the lights by five o'clock; in December by four-thirty.

Gray skies, sagging with snow-heavy clouds, hung over the land. The wind had a knife edge. Morning darkness was not dispelled early and the hours of daylight often seemed short; but there were candles in the darkness: Thanksgiving was one, Christmas was another. Sometimes it seemed that the light shed by the Christmas candle reached around the year.

Mary had been in Boston for several weeks on some business of her own, but she got back a day or two before Christmas. I was glad to have her in the house again for there were so many extra things to do as the holidays approached and I had been waiting for her to help me with them. After she had gone to her room to change for dinner, I began to set the table. Bill came to the dining room to ask me how she looked.

"Oh, she looks fine. Just the way she always does. Bright and cheery."

"She sounds awfully tired. I think you ought to see that she goes to bed early."

"Really? Why, I thought—"

I went to Mary's room and found her sitting in the chair by the fire. Tawn was beside her and she was stroking him. She looked up at me. Her ready smile came to her face, but back of it I was suddenly aware of the tiredness.

"Mary, darling, wouldn't you like to have me bring your supper in on a tray? Get into bed. Be cozy. We'll come in later with coffee and you can tell us all about your doings."

Mary looked at me with surprise, then with relief. It was as if an invisible garment had slipped from her; free of it, she could begin to relax.

"It has been a strenuous time," she said, "and I am really quite tired. How did you know?"

"I didn't. I was just so glad to see you home again that you looked fine to me. Bill knew."

Mary smiled gratefully. "A good long sleep and I'll be ready for anything."

That was the well-nigh infallible remedy for well-nigh anything: one good long night's sleep.

The next morning, after breakfast, Mary and I buckled on snowshoes and started off to the woods for greens. Bill and Tawn stood on the porch and watched us go. The snow was much too deep for even Tawn's long legs, and Bill was going out with Frank to call on the blind people in the area. Frank had put into the car the night before a collection of gifts—toys for the children, boxes of candy, clothes for families where there was need. The car had become a version of Santa's sleigh, but I surmised that what would mean most would be the gift Bill gave of himself—that firm handclasp, that warm tone of real concern, and the gay lilt back of his words.

"How many people is Bill planning to see?" Mary asked.

"Eleven, I think. He hopes to find everyone at home so he and Frank won't have to go out again tomorrow."

"Then he won't be back until late?"

"No. I told him we wouldn't have dinner until seven."

"Let's hope we'll have the house all decorated by the time he returns."

An hour or two later we returned from the woods, our arms filled with hemlock boughs, some spruce, and a few balsam branches. Mary made a spray, tied with a big red bow, to hang on the door; then she placed some of the greens over the pictures in the living room. She lined the Dutch oven recess with hemlock and in it stood the small figure of the Madonna and Child which she had carved from a piece of cherrywood. This was our Bethlehem. To it, many small creatures made a yearly journey. Among them was a gull from Maine, a whale from Nantucket, an owl from Puerto Rico, a pony from the New Forest, a fawn from Germany, a cow from Switzerland, a New Hampshire sheep, a Scottie, a Sheltie, and any number of birds. A motley group they were, gathered from all over the house, made of wood or china, rubber or plaster. It didn't seem to matter that there was almost no difference in size between the rabbit and the whale, and that the patient black tortoise made by the Santa Clara Indians in New Mexico was smaller than the frog that had been carved by a craftsman in Japan.

Mary placed the replica of Linda closest to the Child. "That's the way it should be this year," she said.

While Mary was lining the deep brick arch in the dining room with hemlock, I went upstairs to get the Christmas box. It was a magical time of the year when we did things done at no other time, and brought out as every household did an odd collection of treasures. One of ours was a brown wreath, made from seeds and nuts and cones. It looked lovely hanging on a green wall in the living room. Another was a tiny glass tree which, decked with colored balls, made our centerpiece for the dining-room table. The most cherished treasure, not old but renewed each year, was the tall fat Christmas candle which was placed in a pewter holder in the arch.

When Bill got back he stood in the hallway and breathed deep. We didn't need to tell him what we had done. He knew by the fragrance all around him.

"Did you have a good day?"

"Excellent! We found everyone at home, and we think and hope that everyone is happy."

On the morning of the day before Christmas, Bill and

Frank strung colored lights on the spruce tree that stood north of the house. In the kitchen Mary and I were making spicecakes for our friends. After they had cooled, Mary covered them with white icing, then on each one drew a Christmas tree in green sugar with a brown chocolate trunk.

Bill, coming in for a length of electric cord, said, "If you could only package the aroma in this house it would be as good a present as anything."

Then we made cookies. The recipe was a Danish one that I had used for years at Christmas time. The batter was rolled thin, cut in shapes of fir trees and stars, brushed with egg white and covered with finely chopped nuts and sugar. It was a large recipe. The kitchen was filled with trays of cooling cookies.

The last thing I had to do was stuff the turkey. Mary sewed it up with the neat firm stitches that were one of her trademarks.

"It's going to burst right out of its skin as soon as it gets into the oven and starts to swell."

"Oh no, it won't," Mary patted the plump protuberance. "I've sewed it to hold."

During that week, the mailman had been coming later each day. All along the route, people went out to meet him and take in their arms what would never fit into their boxes. It was also a chance to exchange greetings. In spite of added work, the carrier was more inclined than ever to pass the time of day. His generally impassive face found the way to smile. Everyone smiled. We went into town after luncheon to do some errands and wherever we went people smiled. It didn't matter whether they knew one another or not. The town was gay with Christmas decorations. Carols played frequently over a loud-speaker system from the tower of the Town House.

"It's real, this Christmas spirit," Bill exclaimed. "To me it seems a little more real every year."

"The smiles you see on people's faces make you feel good just to be alive," Mary added.

"Maybe someday the Christmas spirit will wrap itself right around the year."

Bill looked at me as if he were about to say that I was an incurable optimist.

"Oh, Bill, I know that an optimist is often quite as wrong as a pessimist, but there's so much more fun involved!"

"I wasn't going to contradict you, Buttercup," he said. "If there's anything in life that makes one lean toward optimism, it's Christmas."

At the post office we picked up some more mail.

"Cards and cards!" Mary exclaimed. "If just a portion of the wishes they contain come true, we'll all be optimists until Christmas comes round again."

With what remained of the day, Mary and I went calling to deliver the spice cakes. Each one was accompanied by a small potted geranium. I had slipped them several weeks ago and all had taken hold well. They were scions of the geranium which Dan's wife had given me on our first summer. Dug up and brought in to the house every year before frost came, the parent plant had grown through the years and gone on in its slips into many homes.

While we were out, Bill made his telephone calls, checking off one by one the people he wanted to reach with Christmas wishes. Bill had brailled his own directory of phone numbers, both local and out of town. He had been familiar with the dial system for some years, having practiced different methods so he could help other blind people when the dial came to their towns. His own method was to place his thumb and four fingers in the first five spaces,

moving his thumb for six, seven and eight, lifting his hand
and using his index finger for zero and nine. The same was
true for dialing the letters.

Mary and I returned just before twilight, in time for the
year's great ritual—the lighting of the Christmas candle.
Bill smiled at me year after year as I insisted on the ancient rite, but he went along with me.

"It must always be the first light in the house on Christmas Eve." The words went far back in to my childhood. I
could hear my mother saying them, telling me that her
mother had told her about the lighting of the candle when
she was a little girl. It was a family tradition, brought
from the past to be carried in to the future as a part of
Christmas.

I placed a box of matches in Bill's hands. He reached
for the candle to be sure of its height, then felt for the
wick to be sure that it was straight. He struck a match,
tipped it slightly, then with one hand on the candle, moved
the other with the match to the wick. The flame was soon
burning steadily. Bill tossed the match into the fireplace.

"Wish," he said.

Or pray, I said to myself, wondering at a moment like
this if there was any difference.

Then the house lights were lit. White candles had been
placed in the windows that their light might shine out on
the night. Bill flicked the switch that was connected with
the spruce tree on the lawn and the lights came on—red,
blue, green, yellow. They made twinkling patterns on the
snow as wind shivered through the tree. The telephone
rang. It was from the house on the hill across the valley.

"I've been waiting to see your tree lights," a neighbor's
cheery voice said. "Now I can wish you all a Merry Christmas."

"Merry Christmas to you!"

After an early supper we collected a few of our favorite books from which we would take turns reading aloud. We sat by the fire in the living room. Behind us, in the dark dining room, the candle burned steadily, making moving patterns of light and shadow in the red brick arch. It gleamed on the gay wrappings and ribbons of the presents that had been placed there. The fire on the hearth before us was bright and warm. Bill had put on it a huge chunk of maple that would burn well through the night. The room was filled with the fragrance of balsam and spruce.

Mary read the Christmas story from the book of Luke. Known almost by heart as the words were, they sounded with new-old meaning on the night of nights.

Among the reading I had chosen for the occasion was a paragraph from Meister Eckhart, that fourteenth-century mystic who had been speaking to me so much of late—

> " 'While all things were wrapped in peaceful silence and night was in the midst of its swift course . . . a secret word leaped down from heaven, to me. . . . Because the same One, who is begotten and born of God the Father, without ceasing in eternity, is born today, within time, in human nature, we make a holiday to celebrate it. . . . This birth is always happening. And yet, if it does not occur in me, how could it help me? Everything depends on that.' "

Bill had a book in his hand. He held it toward me. "Let's read *Ye Greate Astonishment*," he said.

If the lighting of the candle was my Christmas ritual, this was Bill's. Year after year we had read it until we knew the words almost as well as we knew those in Luke. Mary closed her eyes as I read, but Bill kept his open, looking before him—

> " 'Whosoever on ye nighte of ye nativity of ye young Lord Jesus, in ye greate snows, shall fare forth bearing a succulent bone for ye loste and lamenting hounde, a wisp of hay for ye shivering horse, a cloak of warm raiment for ye twittering crone, a flagon of red wine for him whose marrow withers, a garland of bright berries for one who has worn chains, gay arias of lute and harp for all huddled birds who thought that song

was dead, and divers lush sweetmeats for such babes'
faces as peer from lonely windows—

" 'To him shall be proffered and returned gifts of such
an astonishment as will rival the hues of the peacock
and the harmonies of heaven, so that though he live
to ye greate age when man goes stooping and querulous
because of the nothing that is left in him, yet shall he
walk upright and remembering, as one whose heart
shines like a greate star in his breaste.' "

There was silence in the room, silence in which a candle
burned and green branches gave out fragrance. Then Bill
said quietly, " 'As one whose heart shines like a greate star
in his breaste.' "

"Bill, can you recall that story Dan told us once," I
asked, "of a little town in the mountains that was snowbound one Christmas because of a three-days' blizzard?"

Bill took a moment before he answered. "It was certainly snowbound, but even more than that there had been
sickness in the township and many people had not left
their homes for days. There was little thought of Christmas that year, but one farmer was determined that Christmas should be kept. He hitched his oxen to a lumber sled,
cut down a spruce, and fastened it upright to the sled. He
piled all that his household could spare at the base of the
tree and went from one farm to another, leaving a gift at
every home."

"That must have done something to the people," Mary
said.

"Oh, indeed it did! It broke through something. Dan
told us that one household after another took a kind of
courage from the man with the tree on his sled. They began to dig themselves out of the snow, and then to help
each other make paths through the drifts. By nightfall

they were all able to get to the Meeting House in the town and have a real Christmastime together."

"One heart inspired with giving kindled joy for all," I said.

"Do you suppose it was Dan's father?" Mary asked.

Bill nodded. "I've always suspected that it was, and somehow I think that Dan as a very small boy was on that sled as it made its rounds. I can see him, big-eyed and ready to run whatever errand his father asked of him."

"Dan's story makes me think of the way the Old Masters depicted the Nativity as if it were happening in their own communities," Mary said. "Of course, it is forever happening—the Christmas story. It's like a play in which we all have parts."

"I have a sort of theory," Bill said, "that blessings ride in on our outgoing currents of love and service. That farmer and his family must have had a wonderful Christmas that year, even though their own shelves might have been a little thin."

It was late when we said good night, snuffed the candle, and put the screen up to the fire. Bill let Tawn out, then went around putting out the house lights one by one, often waiting to feel for the cooling of the bulbs. Calling Tawn in and making sure that the doors were latched, he came upstairs.

I leaned on the window sill of my room and looked out at the starry sky and the distant line of hills. There was a sense of wonder abroad that belonged to this one night and to none other in the year. Small marvel that history, song, and story were filled with events that happened on Christmas Eve. Like wildflowers grown from unseen sowing, the legends flourished in the heartground of people the world over. Anything might happen. Creatures might talk, flowers bloom, stars sing. I felt that if I went outside and stood alone in the snowy stillness and listened, I might hear angels singing or animals conversing. It was as if to-night, and always on this one night, the world stood on the brink of some immense discovery. The gift of wonder: perhaps it was the first among the Christmas gifts.

Then The Day itself was upon us with its presents and round of cheer. Friends dropped in. The telephone was warm with long-distance messages. A leaf had to be put in the dining-room table for the Shieling "family." Bill, borrowing Sarah Whin's words the first time we sat down to dinner with her, smiled at all around the table and said, "There's no need for a special blessing, you've blessed this meal by being here." The turkey was crisply brown. The plum pudding flamed. Joy rang the hours of the day un-til near evening when the house became quiet. The candle burned in the arch. The tree lights glittered on the snow. And we three sat down, happily exhausted, to listen to some music.

The week between Christmas and New Year seemed to be a timeless passage of days. It might have been a piece of forever; in retrospect it seemed swift. Our regular rou-tine was discarded. Meals were at any and all hours. Friends arrived; we went visiting. Nothing kept us from giving ourselves to the moment's jollification. One day we had a picnic at the Acre. Tramping over shining white snow well-supported by twenty inches of ice, we found a sunny coign near the High Place where warmth from the sky was reflected by a granite boulder. We lived as if we had nothing to do but enjoy life. We savored our gifts— the new books, the longed-for records, a box of cheese from Wisconsin, a basket of fruit from Oregon. A bee, freighted with nectar and returning to its hive, could have felt no richer than I did just then.

On New Year's Eve we lit the candle in the arch for the

last time. It had burned down so that it was only a few inches high, but the flame was strong and steady and there was enough wax to see the old year out. Bit by bit we put the greens on the fire—hemlock, spruce, holly, mistletoe, balsam. Dry now, they sputtered, crackled, then burst into noisy flame and went up the chimney in smoke. Secretly we made our wishes. Aloud we voiced our hopes.

"With apologies to King David," Mary said, "I've written a Psalm in honor of Year's End."

We were sitting cross-legged on the floor. I moved back to lean against the brick side of the fireplace. Bill shifted his legs so Tawn could rest his head more comfortably against them.

Mary unrolled a scroll upon which she had written her psalm, and read—

"Bless the Lord, O my soul, and all that is within me, bless His holy name. Bless the Lord, O my soul, and forget not all His benefits. Who forgiveth us all our mistakes, who healeth all difficult situations. Who hath surrounded us with all the beauty of New England to enjoy—the glory of starlight, the shining of sun and moon, the twinkling of frost on snow, the unutterable grace of springtime, the rich fullness of summer, the shouting radiance of autumn, the deep quiet of winter.

"Who satisfieth our mouths with good things so that our youth is renewed like the eagle's, and we fly over the countryside on feet or on wheels. We climb up the hills, we swim, we sport and rejoice and sing.

"Bless the Lord, all His works in all places of His dominion—all ye words that move over the paper or from the typewriter, these bless mankind with the inspiration of their love. All ye great thoughts and kind acts and administrations done by the one who fares forth from this household, these proclaim wisdom and mercy. Ye joyous scampering dog, your trust and fidelity and affection do show forth the presence of life. All ye growing things, ye sweet blossoms, delicious fruits and nourishing vegetables, so skillfully tended by the hand of Elizabeth, ye do thrive and grow and sing His praises. Ye patient, inanimate devices which warm us, cool us, refresh and serve us, giving heat, water, protection, so carefully cherished and preserved by the seeing hand of William, these proclaim the unfailing operation of truth. Ye dear, cosy Shieling, blessing all who enter herein, resting, comforting and restoring them, ye do show forth the treasures of the Secret Place.

"O Come, let us sing unto the Lord, let us make a joyful noise. Let us come before His presence with thanksgiving, for the Lord is a Great God and a Great Dear, because He hath given such goodness and blessing and riches into our lives. We cannot number them, they are past all imagining.

"Give thanks unto the Lord, praise His name forever and ever."

When Mary had finished reading she looked at me. Our eyes met and we smiled. Then she placed her hand on Bill's for a moment.

"I think," Bill said, "that the Most High must be very pleased."

We put more of the dried greens on the fire and watched them splutter, then flame and go down to embers. Tiny red lines of burning appeared on the blackened bricks of the fireplace where soot had collected. That was one of the infallible weather signs, that and the cloud-cap worn by the eastern hills.

"Red worms are forming, Bill, first I've seen in quite a while."

He smiled excitedly. "That means snow tomorrow—the more worms the sooner it will come, the brighter they are the better the storm. Are they bright?"

"Oh yes, Bill."

"They're positively vermilion," Mary added.

Bill looked as if he could scarcely wait.

"Remember everybody, we've got to get back to work tomorrow," Mary said, as if to warn us that the holiday season could not go on indefinitely.

Bill turned to me, "Do you recall that night last summer when there were so many kinds of light?"

"M-m," I murmured, "I think so."

Mary nodded. "That's a comforting thought, Bill, when zero is pressing around the house. I remember. It had been a long hot day. The heat was like a heavy hand over the countryside. You, Bill, were away, not getting back until late, and you, Liza, had gone down to the brook. I stayed on the porch."

"Yes, I do—" I had gone across the field and down the slope, stumbling over stones and tussocks in the darkness. Heat lightning quivered intermittently. Superimposed on its fitful flashings were the shapes of clouds. After it, the darkness seemed more intense. The lightning held no threat but served to give brief illumination. I began to see what was around me, and waited between flashes to see more.

The air was cooler near the brook. I sat down in the tall grasses, then stretched out flat on my back to watch the slow appearing of stars. Feeling almost detached from the world, I was bound to it only by the thin hold of the grasses that waved in the slight movement of air following the course of the brook.

In the east a faint spreading of light heralded moonrise. I watched the slow glow widen, and the moon appear— first a slice, then a share, then a round whole. The moon looked surprised, but its expression changed with its color as it rose into the sky. All around me now were shape and definition as moonlight penetrated the night. Meadow growth became distinguishable. Timothy grass stood lower than goldenrod. A clump of black-eyed Susans wore their petals back as if to offer their hearts to the night. The bulk that had loomed high and forbidding a few moments ago was a pine; another mass was a boulder.

The sky at the northerly edge of the meadow was filling with plumes of light. Darkness now seemed to be only an incident, a background for the play of light. The aurora flung itself across the sky in pale shades of green and gold. Wide and constantly shifting, the plumes met for a second at the zenith then moved searchingly across the sky, to subside and be succeeded by other plumes. Each new surge seemed to reach farther, to embrace more.

Then I heard a sound in the meadow grasses. It was not that of an animal—deer, fox, or any other creature—the sound made by one of them would have been sudden, swift, unpremeditated, a moment of exploration and dis-covery, then a journeying on. This was a sound that was careful yet very sure: a tread with seeking in it. The famil-iar sound of footsteps that knew where they were going though they might not always know the way.

"Bill."

"Where are you?"

"Here. In the deep grasses. About ten feet before you come to the brook."

The footsteps approached more slowly. I could see Bill now, his hands a little before him, his arms bent at the elbows. I reached up and caught hold of one of his hands, then I told him all that I had been seeing. He sat down beside me in the grass.

"Remember the night we climbed that little mountain and slept on its summit?"

"Oh, Bill, as if I could ever forget!"

"There was moonrise then, and moonset. There was sunset and sunrise."

"And stars, and stars."

"It was so gentle, wasn't it, the way the light went and came again. So gentle."

After a while we walked back to the house. There was no stumbling over stone or tussock for me now. My arm was on Bill's and his feet knew the way. As we came over the brow of the hill, light from the house reached across the field to us like a hand stretched out in welcome.

But we were in winter now, deep midwinter, and that night of light belonged to the memories of summer.

"How was it you thought of that night, Bill, on this last night of the year?"

"It seemed to me that the Christmas candle brought all those lights into one."

"As it does the year into focus," Mary added.

We waited for the clock to strike twelve and watched the candle as it burned. It would be the last light that we would put out before we went to bed. It had been the first light to usher in the Christmas season.

ELEVEN ✝ *In Light We Walk*

BILL brought in the mail—two letters for Mary, three for me, one for him. I had not heard from Laura for some time, but her first sentence told me that the letter was as much for Bill as it was for me.

"Listen, Bill—" I read Laura's letter aloud. The words seemed to splinter the page on which she wrote for she said that tragedy had struck her home. Her brother was going blind. That was the final verdict of the doctor. There was still a little sight left, but it would not last long.

It was not the first letter of its kind that we had received. I looked at Bill. "You will answer her, won't you, Bill?"

"Of course, I will. Just as soon as I can."

My heart ached for Laura. "I'll get off a line to her today."

I wrote to Laura and told her what I had discovered: "I did not know the world was made of love until Bill lost his sight."

The following evening after supper, Bill dictated to me his reply to Laura's letter. "Elizabeth has told me of the sad news about your brother," he began, and my fingers clicked out the words on the typewriter keys. "I can well appreciate what a terrible shock it must be to him and, of course, to you. I'm sure that you never ceased to hope that something, somehow, could be done to save his sight. But if blindness, according to the doctor, is inevitable, it must be faced and there must be a decision as to how you and he are going to meet it. It is not the handicap that brings limitations so much as it is the mental attitude toward the handicap.

"The first thing I would like to suggest is that you do not overwhelm your brother with sympathy, the second is that you do not let him withdraw from life. This is something, after all, that has to be accepted, but there are within it many opportunities and I would like to help you to see what some of them are."

Bill paused. I had some knitting in my lap and picked it up. The projecting of thought into another area of life was a slow process. He would have had to feel his way in a conversation; he had to do it doubly when the conversation involved a third person and a mechanical means.

"There is the practical side," Bill continued, "and there is the personal. They do their work together. Under the practical, I would urge you to get in touch with your local Association for the Blind. Don't wait until the final moment forces you, but do it now while there is still some sight. Learn through them of the many aids and helps that are available—one of the most valuable being a braille watch. Learn through them of the facilities that lighten the days, and the Talking Book is certainly one. The sound counseling of the Association's social worker is another and, I believe, the most important. Your brother will respond, I am sure, and begin to see that he is not to be denied a life of continuing activity and usefulness.

"Under the personal, let me say first of all to you to keep alive within yourself the realization of all there is still to be enjoyed, still to be done. The period of adjustment which your brother will necessarily go through can be shortened and made less painful if you keep yourself aware of all that yet exists. Treat your brother normally. Include him in your life. That will keep him from going into the depths. It is your own inner light that will help him most during the first dark days." Bill was silent for a moment. "Wait, this isn't the end. There's something more I want to say if I can think of the right way of saying it."

I went on with my knitting.

When Bill commenced dictating again his words came freely. "Your brother will be in a position for a while of having to accept much from others, as a child does, as a person injured in any serious way must. Sometimes, for a grown person, this is hard, often embarrassing. But there is another way of looking at this. He will be giving people a chance to put love into action. Tell your brother to ask for help as naturally as a traveler would ask for directions, and to accept it as unconditionally. All that any one of us really wants to do is to express love, but sometimes it is the most difficult thing. Your brother, because of his present need for help and understanding, is giving an opportunity to people to do just this. You will find in him, I feel confident, a growing initiative and keen interest in his own future. Please let me know how things go."

"Finished?"

"One more thought, but I'd like to add it as a postscript. This is it— I'm enclosing the name and address of the agency for the blind in your locality. Be sure to ask for a visit from one of their trained social workers. It will be of real value to you both."

After Bill had signed the letter he said, "It won't be easy. It can't be for anyone."

"At least he's got her to help him."

"I wasn't thinking of him. I was thinking of her."

That night I lay awake for a long time. Necessity had compelled Bill and me to face a situation and live within its limits. Serene as our life might look to others, lapped in the pleasurable joys of country ways, it had its poignant moments and would have as long as we lived. There were times when I yearned for little things—visual cues, the response to a smile, and the wordless exchange when eyes do the talking.

There were times when, away from home, I longed for the intimacy that writing a letter to Bill would have meant. Bill could write to me, but no letters of mine would be read by him. Even had I learned braille, I knew that I could not convey by the tedious punching of dots the tumult or rapture in my heart. I could send him a lengthy telegram, specifying that delivery was to be by telephone. I could ring him up and be reassured by the tones of his voice. But three minutes always went far too quickly, and even though we became recklessly extravagant and extended the time, it was not like a letter. Words written on a page echo in the heart. The page can be put under a pillow or tucked in a pocket and drawn out to be reread again and again.

No, I could not write to him. I could only say what I felt in spoken words, or be it in useful ways.

"Sometimes I wonder how you see me, Bill. Am I still the same?"

"Oh, no. None of us are. Time is moving on for us all. You're not the same as when you wore that blue dress with the white collar; and yet, in a way you are. It's odd, but I see you less and less as a mental image, and more and more through your qualities. They, rare and precious, are what endure."

I reached out and placed my hand on his.

Looking straight at me and with a quick pressure on my hand he said, "I think I shall never forget hearing a radio interview with the leader of an Everest expedition. Telling why the different men on the expedition were chosen, he explained that one of the key men was chosen because he had, in addition to everything else, selflessness, sympathy, and faith."

Perhaps there were some things that would never be in my life again, but there were new riches that came to me constantly and often unexpectedly. One was on the morning of our wedding anniversary. Waking up in the dim light, that seemed so like the light on that November day in London when we were married, I saw an envelope leaning against the clock on my bedside table. I knew that it was from Bill, and opened it eagerly. His penciled words flowed legibly across the page.

"—this is our day. Quietly I sit here and my thought moves gently back across the years, our years, twenty-five of them the record shows, but surely it has been forever. There have been peaks and there have been valleys, and always your sure feet, strong hands, and valiant spirit have been beside me. Oh, those mountain peaks in Switzerland and Iceland, how they shine! Sometimes the climbs were hard. Sometimes there was a bruise. But what rewards we had! And then for me, one day, the mist thickened in the valleys and even on the mountaintops. For a long, long time it seemed the view was lost.

"Then slowly, feeling your firm hand in mine, through your clear eyes, there came to me an inner sense of light

and almost an outer view. Quietly sitting here, on this our day, I see these things and pray that I may never forget in the busyness of life that you have stood beside me in love, in laughter, and in strength—"

My thoughts went back with Bill's to the mountains we had climbed when we had lived abroad, and to the hills our feet had known since we had come to live in New England. During the days of actual climbing, when we followed rocky trails and our lungs responded to the thin air of the heights, we could not have guessed that one day we would be doing a different kind of climbing. The new ascent was steep and very stony, far steeper for Bill than for me. It was a way of constant adventure, continuing challenge, and always the need was present to master fresh situations. There was nothing I could ever do to

make it less steep, but there were things that I could do all along which would make it less stony.

Mary got breakfast for us on that morning of our anniversary. It was a very special breakfast with cornbread, buttered eggs, crisp bacon, and a coffeepot that filled and refilled our cups. We were talking about mountains and I asked Bill what had been the most thrilling moment to him on one of our Swiss climbs. "Was it the summit?"

"No, actually it was not the summit, though it might have concurred with the summit. It was, after climbing through forests or up a sunless slope, the moment a height was reached where the sun found us. From then on the rest of the way might have been much more difficult, but it was made in light."

"Isn't that what an artist is always striving for," Mary

asked, "that feeling of light which clarifies the whole com-
position and gives it meaning?"

"Does one paint with light?"

"Oh, no!" Mary looked at me, surprised at my question.
"It is the effect of light that matters most."

"Like Blake," I mused, "or El Greco."

"Like the French Impressionists, perhaps," Bill put in.
"I seem to remember that they did a good deal as they
studied the effect of light on their subjects, and even the
color of light itself."

Our discussion led us to Rembrandt and we all agreed
that it was his use of light that revealed not only physical
form but animation within the form. In achieving his ef-
fects, he had kept his lights very light and his shadows
very deep, using halftones to portray detail.

I thought of some of the Rembrandts I had seen in gal-
leries. Recalling them, it seemed as if the character of the
subject stood out in memory as the face stood out on the
canvas. " 'The spirit of man is the candle of the Lord,' " I
murmured.

Mary looked at me quickly. "What made you say that?"

"Thinking of Rembrandt. His portraits. Always the
light seems to come from within."

"Emanation," Mary nodded. "The essence of the person."

Bill pushed back his chair. "It sounds to me as if the
Three-Hours-for-Breakfast Club was in session, and I've
got things to do."

"Oh, Bill, can't we finish this subject?"

"That's just it, you'll never finish it. Continuation this
evening. How about driving me over to Dan's? He
has some ideas about a meeting that's coming up next
week. I'm sure he'll run me home."

"Bill, why wouldn't you let them make you chairman of that committee?"

"You know that, in this case, I have my reasons."

"Yes, I suppose I do. Sorry. I forget sometimes, just the way I can still forget that you don't actually see."

Bill knew his limits and would not take on anything that could only bring frustration.

I drove him over to Dan's then went in to town to do my household shopping. While there, I picked up a startling piece of news which I could not wait to relay to Bill. A small corner of land that seemed a potential natural beauty spot in the center of the town had been sold. A building was to be erected on it. Many people were in a state of excitement, but the fact was brought bitterly home to those who cared that the aesthetic side of life had few to speak in its behalf. A business deal had been made. Money had changed hands. The vantage point that overlooked river and falls had been lost forever.

"Nothing can be done now, Bill. That's what everyone is saying."

"Nothing," he repeated, but his tone was different from mine. "Has anything been started yet?"

"The one small tree that grew there has been cut down. Stakes have been driven in to the ground. I suppose they are outlining the foundation for the new building."

Bill asked who had bought the land, then he asked me for the telephone number. After a lengthy talk with the new owner, I heard Bill urge him to discuss the matter with his partners and then come out to the house.

Late that afternoon, they were all sitting in the living room talking together. It was a complicated situation. The buyers finally agreed to sell the land for the price they had paid for it if a local businessman could be persuaded to sell them a larger lot in a more suitable location. Bill enlisted the help of several friends, and although many difficulties arose an agreement was finally reached. There was a fair sum of money to be raised, but one public-spirited citizen came forward with a substantial loan which enabled the deal to be closed. By the following afternoon, the happily ransomed one-twenty-fifth of an acre was saved: secure in the hands of a committee who were pledged to develop it for the use and beauty of the town.

Dan stopped by with news of the latest developments. "Folks are saying that when the story gets around it may encourage other communities to save their beauty spots." He was standing on the doorstep, letting his eyes range across the hills as I had so often seen him do. "All this pother about a little piece of land and yet, whatever way you look at it, land is the one thing they're not making any more of."

Much later, when Bill had gone out into the field with Tawn, the telephone rang. Sure that it must be for him, I debated calling him before answering; then I decided to take the message and give it to him when he returned.

I recognized the voice as that of a woman who had worked vigorously with Bill to raise the necessary money once the Citizens' Committee had been formed.

"Elizabeth, so it's saved! Really saved . . . No, don't get Bill, just tell him for me how grateful we all are. Only he could have done it. I think there is no one in town more loved or respected . . . It was his selflessness that got people. They were touched by the fact that he worked so hard for something he would never see."

I told Mary what had been said.

"But that's not true about his not seeing! Bill does see, you know that as well as I do," she said stoutly, "and we see more because of him."

"Oh, indeed, I do know that."

Paced to the peace of country ways though we were, there was no escaping the pressures that were part of the present world. Many items I might skip hastily over when reading the paper aloud to Bill, but there was no way of eliminating what came into the house by means of the radio. Perhaps it was no different from what had plagued mankind at various times all through the ages—lack of understanding between nations, complacency, drift, dreadful anxiety, and fear stalking around the edges of life.

And there seemed to be nothing that anyone could do.

Nothing?

Bill was not inclined to accept defeatism whether it involved the state of the world or a small portion of land in a country town.

We three and Tawn had gone over to the Acre to unseal the cabin after its winter of disuse—taking the covers off louvres and chimney and opening it up for a good blow of sharp March air. It was a day that was like a hyphen between winter and spring: neither one nor the other but something of both. We had tramped through the slushy snow in the woods for the pond was rotten with ice breaking up. The surface sagged with great areas of water. There were huge cracks and fissures across it. Every now and then muffled sounds came from it as if it were talking to itself.

After we had done our tasks, we got a good fire going and sat around it waiting for a pail of snow to melt so we could make some tea before we started home. But there was no tea brewed that day that could dispel the sense of utter helplessness I felt just then about the world.

"Listen, Elizabeth, and you, too, Mary, you can't say 'I'm only one, there's nothing I can do,'" Bill looked at us both seriously. "What you should say is, 'Because I am one there is something *I* can do.'"

"That sounds all right in theory, Bill," I muttered.

He shook his head and shifted his feet before the fire. "There are springs in the ground that a man with a witching wand can find," he reminded us. "Remember Kester? The gift such as he has may be rare, but the water is common and is stored for everyone. When the vein is found and put to use, it's there for people to drink, wash with, water their land—whatever, and it won't fail because the vein links to the source. We don't have to understand how it works—"

"*Not* understand?"

"No. All we need to know is that it works for us and with us. It's not understanding that matters, it's trust. And faith asks no questions."

"Bill, you really ought to write your philosophy!" Mary exclaimed.

He laughed. "There's not much to it, not more than would fill two halves of a walnut shell."

"Well, fill one of the halves for me," Mary said.

"If you want to call it a philosophy of life, which sounds much too grand for a few simple thoughts," Bill began, "I'm only doing what everyone does sooner or later, and that is to gather around me a few basic feelings. There are some things essential for living—goodness, brotherly love, reverence for life, thrift, compassion. I'm willing to discard much, because I think that what matters most is simplicity. Innocence might be a better word. Just being. I want to try to prove the little I feel sure of." Bill pushed his chair back as warmth from the fire spread through the room.

The water had begun to simmer in the pail that stood on the trivet. Mary placed the brown teapot near the fire to warm.

"Now, fill the other half for me," I said to Bill.

He was silent for a moment. "You and I have often talked about man's real goal. Whether it is always recognized or not, I believe that it is to find his unity with his Source. If this is so, then every activity, every relationship should become an opportunity to move nearer to that goal."

Bill got up and went to the door to let in Tawn who had been scratching softly at it.

I closed my hand around the two halves of the walnut with all that the shell contained. "Each one of us has to live in the edifice of his own discovery," I said. "The one requirement is that he keep on building."

"With his own tools used to the utmost of his capacity," Mary added firmly.

The water was boiling in the pail. Mary got up and dipped some into the brown pot, then she went to the door and tipped it out. I watched her measure four heaping teaspoons of tea into the pot, then add the now furiously boiling water. She sat down to let the tea draw.

"Then I don't suppose it matters," I said, feeling a sudden and enormous sense of relief, "all these things that are happening in the world and that fill us with anguish and dread."

"Of course, it matters," Bill said quickly, "because life is involved, and life is as sensitive to pain as it is to joy. Because we are aware of that, we should act to protect life. And yet, in a way you're right, it doesn't matter. The question we all have to decide is whether we are standing in the light, or not. If we are, well and good. If we aren't, then it's time we got into it."

The year was turning toward spring. The birds' flutterings were no longer silent. Bursts of song escaped them that increased in volume as the light lengthened. The snow was disappearing fast and green spears of grass had begun to show. Many of the days were gray and cool. There were frequent rains, but when the sun shone it washed the world with warmth. The air was filled with the good clean smell of earth. I went to the woods to see if I could find any evidences of spring. Only the pines and hemlocks were green, their branches offering an invitation to the returning birds.

The woods were filled with the wrack of winter—matted leaves, fallen limbs, retreating snowdrifts. They were bare, and still withdrawn. Then I saw a bee. I watched, and saw another.

They were dropping to the earth and disappearing under some leaves. Emerging a few moments later they went on their way, almost seeming to list with the freight they carried. After the bees had gone I went to the place where I had seen them drop to the earth. Lifting the leaves away, I discovered the first arbutus. It was unbelievable—this minute evidence of the greening, surging life that would soon be all around us. Lifting more leaves away, I found more and more arbutus. The flowers were small and fra-

grant, shell-like in coloring. They seemed as sure of their place in the world, of their reason for being, as had the great redwoods that we had walked under in California.

I picked a few of the arbutus: enough to put in Bill's hands for him to smell, for him to know that once again another spring was at our door.